The Library
Union Street

94c

SOMERSET
COUNTY LIBRARY
3 1681199 1

LETTERS FROM A SOLDIER

MHAIRI MILLIGAN

Copyright © 2017 by Mhairi Milligan.

Library of Congress Control Number: 2016921307
ISBN: Hardcover   978-1-5245-9634-7
           Softcover   978-1-5245-9633-0
           eBook   978-1-5245-9632-3

All rights reserved. No part of this book may be reproduced or transmitted in any form or by any means, electronic or mechanical, including photocopying, recording, or by any information storage and retrieval system, without permission in writing from the copyright owner.

Any people depicted in stock imagery provided by Thinkstock are models, and such images are being used for illustrative purposes only. Certain stock imagery © Thinkstock.

Print information available on the last page.

Rev. date: 01/17/2017

To order additional copies of this book, contact:
Xlibris
800-056-3182
www.Xlibrispublishing.co.uk
Orders@Xlibrispublishing.co.uk
738696

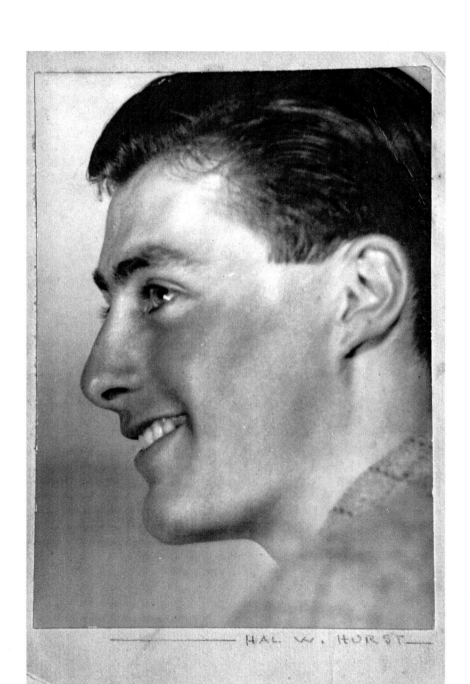

The Bridesmaids, Sheena Bone and Mhairi Falconer

BEFORE

It was very hot at the end of August 1940 when we came down to London for the wedding of my sister Sheila at St Marks, North Audley Street. She was marrying Alan Kilpatrick, a lovely man, always known as Tiggy.

I was to be a bridesmaid and she had promised me a splendid usher. And indeed he was! At the reception at Claridges, we sat and talked all afternoon. "Are you nursing?" he asked. I had to admit I was still at school but refrained from saying I was only 14.

My father asked him to stay to dinner – all excitement with Somerset Maugham sitting at a nearby table. Again we talked and talked. More excitement when the family retired to bed and the bombs started falling. It was the start of the blitz.

Next day Tiggy's brother Bob got married at Thames Ditton where both the Kilpatricks and John lived.

Again we talked and talked sitting in their beautiful garden. He was just going to join the army and we agreed to write to each other, not knowing we would not meet again in over five years. These are some of his wonderful letters. He fought at Alamein, Sicily, and won the DSO in Italy.

He and two close friends, Tom Davis (who won the M.C.) and Roy Heckscher, were known as my Three Musketeers.

Reading the letters now makes me realize how my early letters were those of a 14 year old and it is fascinating to watch him fall in love with a mythical person.

9th September 1940. From Woodside Weston Park, Thames Ditton

My dear Mhairi,

How do you do. I hope I have spelt your name right, it looks terribly Australian or do I mean New Zealandish? I am writing this on top of the gramophone which is playing the ballet *Coppelia* with tremendous enthusiasm, it don't 'arf make a noise! Well my address in case I forget, is this: Gunner Butler JC, (that's me), 939010,207AA battery, R.A.Training Regiment, Devizes, Wiltshire.

I'm not really at all sure if this is right and it may be a vital secret, but if you should cast a pearlish letter before my swinish self, I hae nae doot it will arrive. That last expression is Scottish and is to be compared with "Scots Whahae", which I always thought was a sort of hearty way of saying Howya Scots?

I will now interrupt this almost unbelievably dull epistle to ask you a few questions, e.g.: did you arrive safely after the wedding? Have you been bombed to pieces? Have you noticed how rapidly the flowers are withering now? The last question you can no doubt imagine, so I won't aggravate you just yet by asking it. Anyhow, the sum of these questions is this: I hope, my dear madam, you and your parents arrived in safety and are now flourishing (unlike the flowers). I have composed a brilliant tune worthy of our friend the poet and easily superior to The Nightingale. The words are simple and so is the tune. The words are these:

"as a man might say to another as he trod on a biscuit tin." The brilliance of the thought must be plain to you.

I have also envisaged a vast poem dealing with the state of affairs after the war. The only two lines as yet translated into words are these:

I dare say your girl will be as fair,
And the stars be as bright in the night of her hair.

Infinitely touching, wouldn't you say? The night of her hair is sheer genius.

The horrid Germans have been bombing London, as you know. They pass over our heads and the guns go off at them and the guns are ever so horrid too. The guns near us are 4.7s and you can hear the shells scream through the air. It makes much more noise than a bombsk. (There's a wee rhyme about three boys at the Grammar School Omsk who manufactured a horrible bombsk, but I can't remember it. I should be grateful if you could tell me it, but doubt if you can believe I made it up myself – it's all very trying.)

And we see that the fires started in London which light up the whole sky. Life is much too noisy and exciting. The other day we were on a housetop in our capacity as LDVs, when a plane came throbbing over. All the searchlights converged on a spot directly over our heads and a perfectly beastly plane dived straight down with a horrid tearing sound. I thought it had been hit and started up a bar or two of Rule Britannia, (never could spell that word), but what it actually did was drop a couple of salvos of bombs. Fortunately they fall ahead of the plane and actually landed about half a mile away from us, but it was all very tiresome especially as every gun in the vicinity opened fire and we'd got no tin hats. However, we stood vaguely behind a chimney pot and when a few more guns had gone off and a flare or two had been dropped and a British fighter appeared, there was comparative calm. I think the plane got away.

I was up in London on Friday and they had dropped some parachute flares. They came down in threes like stars and hardly moved at all, they came so slowly. There were three over the Thames as we crossed over Westminster Bridge. They lit up the H of P etc, it was super.

I can't end gracefully on this tiny piece of paper so I shall have to commence a new sheet which is silly really as I shan't know quite what to say upon it, however.

I haven't seen Sheila and Tiggy but they rang up to say they were still in one piece. I had hoped to see them before I went but as the train service to London is at present in a somewhat interrupted state, I hear I shall be unable to do so. I have got to write to my ex-housemaster and others dammit. That should have been a new paragraph but one really cannot afford luxuries like that. I can't think of anything more to say. Do you still think I'm horrrrible? Mr Kil[1] is as red as ever and still embraces everyone within range (of the female sex) with his customary relish. I haven't seen Cleve Mitchell[2] but doubtless he still thinks your eyes are like liquid depths of Azure, or wasn't that what he said?

I once got a thing out of the machine on the pier which said something like *"Her to Him, or what your future lovely thinks about you"*. I think I must have got Him to Her by mistake because the person concerned wanted to dive into the liquid depths of the azure eyes of his future lovely.

My only other adventure with machines was one entitled "test your sex appeal". On my inserting the halfpenny and pulling the lever, a horrible card shot up from the bowels of the machine saying 'harmless'. So I burst into tears, and resigned myself to fate and bachelordom.

It's going to rain and I've got to cycle 10 miles to see someone. Isn't life hard? I've now adequate space to make an elegant ending, but as I never know quite how to make an elegant ending it doesn't really matter. May I express the wish that the flowers may cease to wither in your sight, that you may be spared the grim sound of time's winged chariot hurrying near; that your age may cease to worry you as it merely means

---

[1] Tiggy's father Mr Kilpatrick

[2] One of Mr Kilpatrick's business partners

you have longer to live – (always supposing you aren't hit by a horrible Bombsk – Ha! Ha!).

I may in short wish you everything you wish yourself. Well, all the very very best of everything Mhairi, and don't be good.

John

PS I haven't forgotten about the lorries and will endeavor to get transferred to Scotland as soon as possible.

                                              Subsection A
                                                A Battery
                                           07 AA___ regt RA
                                                 Devizes

[These are the only envelopes I've got]

Thursday 18th or 19th September 1940
I'm not sure which

My dear Mhairi

    Thank you so much for your charming letters. I'm writing this in bed by the way so it will no doubt be illegible. Well, well, well, talk of my letter being typical, yours had 57 exclamation marks in it. I refer to the first letter which I received yesterday; I haven't dared to count the second one. Really, Mhairi, you are certainly, it seems, incurably romantic; in fact you made me roar. I feel singularly devoid of inspiration and with having had a horrible time marching up and down the square all day. Nay of a truth ' tis ten mins past ten of the clock and as "lights out" is at 10.15 I shall terminate this epistle tomorrow if these accused militarists suffer me to be in peace for more than 2 minutes at a time.

Well, I'll tell you what's happened since I left my home in years gone by: at least 6 years it seems. We took 14 hours to get down here having to stop every now and then while someone repaired the rails which had been removed by the force of Germanic bombs. I had a hot discussion with a cleric who was shaped like a peacock. We had to wait for hours at every station. Horrribly boring. Anyhow we got here eventually. There are quite a few Cambridge (and Oxford) people here which is lucky as the average recruit comes from Stepney and while being no doubt an excellent fellow, is a little tiresome. The height of his humour is to come into the barrack-room and shout out "all on parade". Nobody takes the slightest notice: the humorist tears his sides with laughter and all his pals join in. This happens regularly four or five times a day. The result is that occasionally there really is a parade and everybody roars with laughter and fails to appear. E.g. the other day I was having a bath. I had just got in and someone came in and said "Parade". As it was a reliable man I leapt out of the bath, dried, etc and was 3/4 dressed when he said 'sorry, no parade".

Re-enter bath. Relax. Utterly content with life for once. Re-enter friend "Sorry, there is a parade". Me, skeptically, "Go away and don't be a silly little boy: Uncle John's staying in his bath!" Which he did and was very late on parade. All very tiresome. All the people who have been in the O.T.C. have been formed into one squad. We go out to defend England home and beauty (especially beauty) when the Jerries land. It is very difficult to get leave and we have been told we've no hope for at least 2 or maybe 3 months. My one ambition at the moment is for this nameless war to end. We get into Devizes itself about once a week but there's nothing to do there except pub crawl. So we accept the inevitable and crawl. Today we get paid – big thrill. I have now to parade for hours, so temporarily farewell my luve (Scottish)

It is now 8.30 p.m. and we are free. I have just eaten some baked beans on toast. They cost 4d with a cup of tea. Tomorrow we have an inspection of a sort. Damn. I am now sick of trying to describe life in this hole.

It harnesses my worst passions and I crawl round on all fours snarling horribly and eating treacle out of a pot. So enough. To your letter – so I am disturbing am
I? That sounds excruciatingly funny to me. Mhairi I believe you are a flirt. No, I am sure you are a flirt. As I re-read your letter I came across the most violent insinuations surrounded by battalions or batallions, no, battalions, of exclamation marks. Do keep it up. It's most encouraging, charming and nice and maybe I'll be transferred to Edinburgh yet. Anyhow I'll come up and roll in the heather next spring on 3 conditions. One, that you ask me, one that I get leave, and one that we are still living – in that order.

Once more I am in the predicament of having begun a new page. What shall I say thereon. I hope you enjoy your school. What is its address that I cannot write direct to you, varlet poetess? Which reminds me – I refuse to have you equal your humorous verse with my classic gem: The two lines are now completed thus:

I dare say your girl will be as fair,
And the stars be as bright in the night of her hair,
And her mouth's kisses will be as warm,
And the storm of her conquest the same swift storm.
I am not sure about the last line!

I have decided incidentally that the army is very badly run. I could do much better. I could make people get up at 9 instead of 6. This is incidental.

Surely you can get some inspiration for your novel. Such a charming idea for a plot, Mhairi, let's get married on Monday, shall we? I am now in the quandary of having no more to say. I am so honoured that you dreamed about me. I bet you can't really remember what I look like. As a matter of fact I dreamed about you but you weren't very nice and you had the most queer collection of friends imaginable. I woke up chuckling. As by the way you say you know me quite well, it would be so interesting if you told me quite straight – I can take it, sister – what I am like. Yes, it really would be interesting; do oblige me, Mhairi deeaarr.

Well I don't suppose you will get this letter for about a week as it takes 6 days to get home from here and that's only about 1/5 of the distance. But please do write as I love to have your letters. They lighten this execrable existence considerably. And oh my love do be a bad girl at school and don't do a stroke of work and do continue to be incurably romantic. This not-very-avuncular advice is a sure recipe for the sack so take it or leave it.

I don't think this is at all an interesting letter, but at least I haven't yet asked you to knit me a pair of trousers. Well I hope you enjoy life and do write.

Love John

Subsection AA
BATTERY 207TH
AA TRAINING REGIMENT RA,
DEVIZES
WILTS

October 3rd 1940

My dear Mhairi,

I don't think it's Thursday, really, and I don't suppose it's October 3rd. I'm in bed feeling as dumb as ever. Someone has just said I'm a quiet fellow, with which I have hastened to agree. Really they are the most awful people in my room. They are all dreadfully public school and say 'Old Boy' in the most bored tones imaginable and of course they play cards and drink and swear and spit. Which reminds me I had an 'orrible thick night last night and have had wool in my mouth all today.

We managed to get a pass into Devizes and thought we ought to celebrate the fact.

We've had a fatuous psychological test which is meant to test your ability for specialized jobs. I call it fatuous as I did very badly. I'd like to think my mind is more philosophic than arithmetical. You had to do things like this: the Officer says *"on the paper in front of you are three squares. Now if a tank is bigger than a motorcycle, don't put two crosses in the third square, but if a Colonel is of a lower rank than a lieutenant put a double ring in the square nearest to the left hand side of the paper."* And that is not very exaggerated. As I say, I didn't do very well at all, so you will understand why I belittle the test. Much to my surprise, however, I shot a good target the other day, so it evens things out.

This again is not very interesting, so let me to your beautiful letter. As far as I remember your birthday is in October and I should plump for the 23rd. And to think that you have only had 14 of them. My God, I think I told you before that you will undoubtedly die young! Anyhow I hope your 19th birthday will be a happy one.

These people really are a dull lot. I do not like the army and I think must try to get transferred to the RAF, but I can't be bothered to write and try. It's now going to be lights out, so I'll bid ye guid nicht, (scots) .

I expect you've noticed very dirty marks across the paper every so often. That's because I've very dirty hands, covered in bluebell to be precise.

Well once more to your letter. It's no use my even attempting to achieve your high level of endearing epithets. And please do forgive me, (wonderful though I am), for not taking you too seriously. Was my letter romantic? You must quote me the purple passages! Before I forget I must congratulate you with all my heart on only having one at a time. It sounds most sinister, please carry out your threat and shock me since I have always wondered what it is like to be shocked.

Now listen Mhairi, just what does this sort of a sentence mean? *"But of course we are completely different in that respect, so you wouldn't know !!! "* I quote verbatim. *Of course I quite realize that you are potty, but wondered if there is any other explanation.* And as far as your feminine wiles to discover the date of my birthday, well, well well I'm surprised at you. Be a little man or a lady and tell me just what month is to provide you with the perfect husband and I will divulge my deep secret. I shall drop off to a fevered sleep any minute now. Give my love to the Bunnies at your next meeting.

The only view that I ever get is that of barrack huts – monstrous, you know, monotonous.

It's now Friday. My headache has gone but I have a blister. It rains. In a minute or two we have a ceremonial parade. After that we again wait in the rain to be interviewed by the major. C'est la vie.

A rumour is circulating the parade is not until 9 so we will none of us get ready and a Sergeant will come in at 8.25 and say "Why are you not on parade"? (at least that's the gist of what he'd say). C'est la vie. I've no more to say. It's now after lunch and we have had ceremonial. The colonel and I had the following conversation.

Colonel 'Ah, tall chap, how tall are you?'
Me: '6'4" sir.' which I'm not
Colonel 'father a tall chap?'
Me '6'4" too, sir'.
Colonel 'what are you in civil life?'
Me 'Undergraduate at Cambridge, Sir.'
Colonel 'oh, what college?'
Me 'Christ's, Sir'
Colonel 'Ah. What sport do you play?'
Me 'hockey and cricket, sir'
Colonel 'don't row, what?'
Me 'no sir'

Colonel passes on twirling his moustaches.
C'est la vie, Mhairi my dear. Well farewell my romantic one, and may your dreams come true

With love from John

PS I haven't got a photo

October 15th   939010   B Battery
                                    207a AA Try.Regt.RA
                                    Devizes WILTS

My dear Mhairi,

But how sweet of you. They fit like a glove. Ha Ha. They arrived yesterday, a labour of love. I wore them on guard last night, so you have the comforting thought of having been a great comfort to a troop.

N.B. Before I forget, the change of address. I am now in B Battery and am about to learn something about AA gunnery which is pretty good for the Army. However I hear that 3 weeks out of the 4 are spent doing fatigues so I shall probably be a better spud peeler than gunner.

It is now Wednesday afternoon. On Monday I was on guard all night, but last night I should have been on Fire Picket all night but got a substitute and all today I have been cleaning up the Sergeants" Mess which consists of doing very dirty things with left-over food. In fact we have only been let out for an hour till 4 o'clock then we return. Definitely I shall be a housemaid nonpariel when t'war is finished.

Well Mhairi. I'm afraid it is now Monday morning. To be precise a lecture is in progress. But the point is that I'm absolutely bung full of apologies. I fear your Scottish ire at my long delay in the writing of this letter and I hardly dare continue to plead overwork. But alas tis true. Life is very trying.

Damn this letter – it's getting out of hand. Which is bound to happen when you come to think of it, if one writes about 3 lines per diem (Latin). The enclosed tiddly - what is rather beastly but it's all I could get in this town forsaken of the Deity. Anyhow I wish you very many happy returns of your birthday, your 19th birthday, and have no doubt you will continue to increase in beauty, wit and charm and grace (pretty compliment, that). Moreover as I have been so long in answering your letter and thanking you for the mittens, I will now be good and answer some of the questions you asked – some! My birthday is in July, so I'm not more than 8 years older than you. I shall have to leave this letter in a very few minutes in order to go out and endure some form of unpleasantness till 5 o'clock. I have even endured to have a photograph of myself taken but I am hoping it will come out as photos of myself always embarrass me no end. (N.B. My usual apologies for not taking you seriously but I am improving, aren't I?) I have now arrived at the quoted songs. Well well well. I am shocked to the core.

Well (excuse all the wells) my heartless one it is now the evening and the afternoon was not too bad. So let me refer once more to your letter. You're quite potty. I think I told you that before, but as you probably realize it by now it doesn't much matter but just why was it typical of me (my dear!) to give you a mulberry? Were you confusing it with a raspberry. But the giving of that particular fruit is a lady's privilege. So what have you?

    I am very worried indeed about this letter as it is horribly (only 2 rs as it's wartime) feminine and all confused and has no point anyhow. The destruction of my soul by the army method is a great point of bitterness with me. Yesterday we played hockey against the G.W.R and won. I scored 117 goals. We all got tight after it and someone was sick in the bar. Horrrible. Which reminds me –how did your concert go off. My name is Cluhertabarthock (pronounced Clutterbuck). My friends from Cambridge go under the following names: Meikle, Gray, Chapman, Musson and a few more whose names I can't recall. Some of them are v. some quite and some not very nice. I'd no idea about Jimmy and Elsie. I hope they get on alright. I expect they will as they're both crazy as well. In fact I am developing a theory that everybody is crazy – everybody nice I mean. What are you like? Well I refuse to say as you would not believe it in any case. (Sinister remark that as you don't quite know what I mean, do you?) What was the incident that the ludicrous song referred to? Hide nothing from me. I am Wahula Wahula, the amazing seer of all things. Wowula, calubrahadan. I am now casting a spell (spell.....). It is all plain to me of course as your phraseology doesn't give even dense chap like me much chance of failing to understand. Oh woman! I am now going to fill my frame with fodder, I have just had a hot bath and feel better than I have felt in all my 6 years of army life.

    My beautiful poem was still-born I'm afraid as it is of course impossible to write poetry when one's soul is destroyed. A pity because it had great promise. I was to have included the purple heather of Scotland.

I must end to eat. Do have a happy birthday and do enjoy life. I'm sure you do.

With love

John

November 10th 1940

B Battery
207th AATry Regt A.A.
Devizes WILTS

My dear Mhairi,

I'm terrrribly sorry for having been such a terribly long time in writing but the trrrrouble is this perfectly horrrrrible photograph which was (and I'm hardly surprised) a complete failure on the first attempt. Apart from this we have been inundated with generals and things and people keep rushing about and saying "clean that window" – which having been done they say "Reclean that window".

Generals are a plague. I think the chief trouble is that they don't arrive to time. Consequently the Powers that Be here can't arrange a programme for them. The result, admirably demonstrated yesterday, is that we go out in the morning as usual. We are then sent back to put on anklets. We are then sent back to take off capes because it is raining and if we kept our capes on we would keep dry. The next move is overcoats on (because it happens to be rather warm) and anklets off. We are then dismissed once or twice and prepared for ceremonial parade which never comes off. Finally the general appears and creates such consternation that people are just rushed about the place and told to do jobs they've never done before. The general fortunately is a) much too polite, b) for too disinterested and c) much too ignorant to notice anything and beams on us all. Isn't it fantastic?

The rest of B and D Batteries are moving off to a Practice Camp on Tuesday but I don't know what will happen to the Potential officers. I fear we will remain here for a month at the very lest. Excuse all this shop. It is quite inexcusable but only goes to show you how the army destroys your soul as I have said in every letter. I always think of my soul as a pancake in the shape, roughly, of a foot. I know it is very childish so you needn't bother to tell me. Well fortunately as you no doubt know, being such a well informed person, I take

huge sized feet – I mean shoes – so my soul is correspondingly large. Supposing therefore that my soul was size 12 a the beginning of my army career and supposing that 3 men dug ¼ acre per day 3 feet deep, how long would it take the bath water to run away assuming that there was no plug. I believe I told you there was madness in the factory, I mean family. Here it rains every day! Presumably it does chez vous as it always rains in Scotland anyway.

I refuse absolument to answer your questions. And as for the insinuations – I think I remarked about them before. It occurs to me at this point that you will be entirely unable to read the letter but I am lying in what is said to be a bed and I'm half dead. I can hardly bear to send the photo. It is so very silly. However. I have just been playing poker at which I contrived to lose 2/-. Just think of it – almost a day's pay.

I presume you are as bored at school as I am here, O old woman or aren't you ever bored? If it weren't so near the end of the paper I should at this point tell you what you were like – sorry, what I think you are like. What a pity! Anyway I told you once. Poor Sheila. I am sorry to hear what an awful time she keeps having. London must be in a bit of a mess I imagine.

Well sweet lady I take of you a regretful farewell but shall certainly fall asleep any minute now.

With love and enjoy yourself!

John

November: 24th   E Section
                                         D Battery
                                            207th AATrug Regt AA

My dear Mhairi,

    I am manning which is annoying. Yesterday we were manning too but I got off that to play Hockey. The Regimental Hockey team would make you laugh. We have never lost a match and I doubt if we ever will. If the other side looks to be a good one we severely wound all its leading lights and every time the umpire gives a foul against us we all shout and scream and sweat and offer to fight him. I am not exaggerating. Yesterday was the culminating point. Their forwards scored rather a good goal in the first ten minutes so we set about terrorizing them and our centre forward who is a sergeant might hit one of their men on the seat with his stick and our captain who is a Lieutenant and might have been expected to "er play the game, cads" rushed round saying rude words and whirling his stick around the place. We won 5.3 eventually although we only had 9 men. The man who was meant to play outside right left for a firing camp 3 weeks ago but the captain hadn't noticed and half way through another chap left to catch a train. Silly isn't it?

    It is now afternoon when Christian folk should be sleeping. We are still manning. Manning by the way means that you get up at an unearthly hour and report on the gun park and having tested all the guns, predictors and other instruments in the dark and done some drill, sit about in a so-called pavilion until a message comes through that a million Germanic aeroplanes are advancing whereupon someone shouts through a microphone "Manning Party close on Gun (pronounced goon) Sights". It's really rather a waste of an afternoon when one ought to be washing socks and things. I do hate washing socks and keep putting it off from day to day until my kit bag is full thereof.

Did you ever meet Kit Garnett? He is one of Mr Kil's partners and is a 2nd Leiut. down here. I went out to dinner with him. He has a terrific house near here and you can't imagine the thrill to be had from eating off china plates and drinking out of a glass! He was at Bob's wedding by the way so you may have seen him there. He's a frightfully nice chap.

I liked your eulogy of the young heroic soldiers. You ought to see some of the specimens we get here. They couldn't really help being called up anyway (subversive talk: 5th column: extreme cynicism – forgive me honey). Sweet young men. I'm glad too that you liked the fair maidens of Girton. They were a bit of a pain in the neck when I was up (the very few that I knew of course) but everybody knows that England is going to the dogs and isn't what it was when everybody was young.

By the way (why am I for ever saying by the way? It's a more tiresome thing, indeed yes). Tell me what time of day or night you wrote pages 4-6 of your letter. Must know. Must. Must know. I just love your underlinings but don't like your favorite tunes very much. It strikes me that Miss Susan Davidson must have wonderful taste (seven exclamation marks). Going further down the page I find I am a tired soldier. The psychological effect of this has been tremendous and for the last four days I have been trotting around on all fours – verily a bearlike sight. I am practically asleep and would be were it not so cold. There is a fool who is arguing foolishly nearby and I keep getting drawn into it, malgre moi (French) (sorry.)

You know Mhairi I shall one day write you a long and serious letter. Wouldn't it be fun? For instance I could say you were everything your father read out as being Bob's wife's attributes (if you see what I mean) or almost anything.

We have just had an air raid warning though as far as raids go we have not been bothered much. I still wonder what I'll think of London as I hope to get leave in about 3 weeks time. It won't arf be nice to see nice people again – you'd better come down from your far wild mountain haunts and cast the sun of your presence on our southern vales as one might say. Hate to think how angry you'll be at not being told what you're like once again! Ha!!!!ha!!!!!!!!

Curse this war: isn't it an awful waste of everyone's time.

Cheerio, love John

December 12th (1940)　　　　E Section
　　　　　　　　　　　　　　2 Battery
　　　　　　　　　　　　　　207thAA.Tong Regt

My dear Mhairi,

    Thank you so much for your letter. Don't they take years in these sad days in which the world totters on the brink of chaos, where the gloom dragon shows its disastrous face (etcetera). I have had a difficult morning. Very difficult morning. I am what is known as a room orderly. Now this means that you look after the room and keep it tidy. In point of fact I am quite incapable of keeping anything tidy, but the post implies that you do not go on parade all day. Well as the first parade was at 7.45 and as it is extremely cold and grey and horrid and miserable at 7.45, and as this parade was Physical Training, and as you have to parade for Physical Training in gym shorts and vest and greatcoat (which means your legs get frozen if nothing else does) – well, after all those "ases" you will understand why I put up a tremendous fight against heavy odds to get the job of room orderly . I didn't clean any of my bit, I stayed in bed late, meandered over to breakfast at my ease whistling happily to myself and saying what a fine life the army really was and how pleasant it was to get up early on a cold dark misty day and walk across a cold dark misty parade ground to eat a cold dark and misty sausage for breakfast. Very well. See now and harken to the tale of woe and the manner in which a young man's pride was punished. I return from my breakfast and find a howling mob of unpleasant soldiers, utterly unappreciative of the glory of the dark misty morning feeling, who scream out in discordant voices that the fire has gone out, and why the hell etc. I must explain that we have no form of central heating in our hut and the fires were put in in a vain endeavor to dry up the streams of water which flow in whenever it rains. Well we pinch some coke from one placed or another and so, usually, keep it going continuously, or continually. Some nameless fellow had let it burn out, but in my large hearted way I forgave him and amidst the jeers and conflicting advice of all 60 members of the room, I began to build a fire. It's a sort of closed stove of a very ancient pattern and one can't get at its inside properly to lay wood on. I thought "How annoying" and then realized I hadn't any wood. Well I searched outside in the dark cold air and at last found some which I then realized to be wet. Still my temper was unruffled. I ventured a mild "damn". I had a brilliant idea. I ran to a neighbouring sleeping hut and took one of its blackout boards which I broke up. Very well. Still amidst the advice of those standing round, I began to screw up paper and drop in wood. I then laid a few bits of coke on top and fetched some burning coke from a nearby fire. In I dropped it and then quickly put some wood and more coke on, opened the bottom and waited confidently whistling "a bachelor gay am I". Yes the army was a good life. I turned away to sweep up some of the filth off the floor. Suddenly more discordant howling informed me that the fire had gone out. I don't know how. My sang froid was a little upset. I think I ventured to say 'blast' that time. After I had remade the fire 3 times my language became rather stronger and the army seemed as bad as it has ever been.

I thought "why did I take on this job". I pushed this base thought from my mind and put on a smile to show that it didn't really bother me a bit making up a fire four times by an apparently foolproof method and seeing it fail utterly each time. Imagine, fair reader, the comments passed by my comrades. I left the --- fire. I discovered the dirty laundry had to be taken down to the Battery Office and the clean laundry fetched. All the dirty laundry and all the clean laundry. So this meant a list of all 60 members of the room . I made it. I went down to the office. It was shut. I waited. I left it and as I had just arrived back at the Sleeping Hut I was told "You must go and take the dirty laundry". I gave the speaker my rough opinion and his face, his father's and mother's face, his habits, the state of his health and what I hoped the future would bring. I then went down to the office and had to sort out the dirty laundry. Then I had to sign for each one. There were 60, fair reader and I had to sign for each one. The process was repeated for the clean laundry. I returned at last wearily, broken, a ruined, exhausted man. The sergeant told me to line up the bits and get everything tidy and wondered in no mean terms why I hadn't done it already. I was silent. One cannot give one's opinion of a sergeant's face, habits and antecedents. After all that I started on the stove again. Someone suggested that you couldn't light a fire with coke. Someone would take ¾ of the morning to suggest that. I went to the coal dump and I fetched some coal. The fire is now roaring and I sit by it in a hopeless condition writing this, probably, almost certainly the last manuscript I shall ever write. I tried to bring off a triumph. I said "Look at the lovely fire, boys; just a little patience needed. Leave it to John and all will be well." But they didn't agree, the ungrateful beasts. P.T. in future will hold no terrors for me. I will go on every parade that is ever held. I will do anything, but I will no be room orderly, no, never. But one thing I have learnt. <u>You can't make a fire with coke.</u> The army is awful, the room is awful, the day is awful, the people are awful, the prospect is awful – BANG! (I have shot myself).

Who was it, who said I was a tired soldier! Oh boy oh boy oh boy, what a war, what a war what a life.

As you now have some idea of my mental state I will tell you there's no news I can give you We are not able to get leave until we have had an interview for entry into an O.C.T.U and as no one knows (as usual) when this will take place, I don't know when we'll get leave. I see in the papers that the army is to have Roast Beef instead of Turkey, but don't tell anyone, we've been having it 6 days out of 7 for the last 13 weeks, so it'll make a nice change. Actually unless we are very unlucky I think we'll get leave over Christmas. I sincerely hope so.

It's really very sweet of you to knit me a sock. Made me roar when you asked what size I take. You'd better unpick it and start again as I take a 12! Shall refuse to write serious letter. Perhaps as I lie a-dying! I have just reread your epithets on yourself. Tut tut, how can you? Yes I read Classics and admit its rather funny and I hope you did brilliantly in all your exams and do tell me where you came in all your exams and what the average age of your form is (hm. Sore point) and then I can find out how stupid you really are (hm. Dirty one) Also tell me about your entertainment of the school. It sounds too too scintillatingly brilliant, my dear, what? But what unholy joy at missing church. Tut tut child. Child hm. I am frantically jealous of Tig's stripe.

Will post this before shooting myself again. All ze best and love from John

The Usual Hole
December 24th 1940

Ravishing female, gorgeous child
(Ha! I bet that makes you wild!)
Thanks a million for the lovely lamby scarf

Lamby is my own word and is pronounced with a 'b' and <u>not</u> 'lammy'.

Truly sweet, twas good of you. It's a beautiful objet d'art. Chez d'oeuvre, cul de sac and coupe Jacques etc.

I am sending you some handkerchiefs which is most uninspired but I never know what to get for females (or felines), so you must take pity as my poor masculine ignorance and accept them with my love. I am hoping they'll reach you by New Year's Day seeing as how you are a Highland Lass. That sounds either like a pub or a tobacco. I loved your card. Do give Tiggy a kick in the pants when you see him and say I have been meaning to write and ask him how he likes being a troop. I am always full of good intentions you know. And do give my love to Sheila and your mother and father. Herein I wish to the

Falconer family a most happy and cheerful new Year. Wha'cha auld ghoulie (Irish-American).

I do envy you, you know. I am going on leave tomorrow I think so am very pleased. Had hoped to get home for Christmas, but the army being the sort of thing it is, they don't do things in a logical way. That is an extremely restrained statement of fact as for about a week I have been ranting in large phrases about the Injustice of Things.

You seem to do the most incredible things in your academy. I thought it was only the Girls' Own that eager girls went out at night in dressing gowns. I feel tempted to ask whether you found the villainous maths mistress up there on the roof making forged bank notes and at the Tummel Falls Sue should have fallen in and you should have dived 50 ft and to a flat rock and carried her limp form for 5 mins back to the school. Did you?

I feel it behoves me to request you dear Madame to convey to Sue[3] my most kindly regards and wishes for a happy New Year as she takes such a kindly interest in the curriculum of me (Chinese).

This is a horrid little letter but I request you, wee lassie, to forgive me for that I have an orful lot to do before going on leave (always supposing I do go). Christmas time was really quite fun.

---

[3] my school friend

So fare thee well my best and fairest or is it dairest? And don't lose heart over the continual fading of the flowers.

With love,

John

Same delectable spot
Wednesday Jan 15th

My dear Mhairi,

Thank you so much for your scintillating last letter which I am very late, I fear, in answering. I seem to have had a riotous week-end which is pretty rare in the army as you may have gathered by now. Someone started it by having a 21st birthday party which was very pleasantly reminiscent of Cambridge. After that we seemed to spend an enormous quantity of money one way and another with the result that I am now eating as much of the army food as possible whereas before I aristocratically ate in my own time a the Y.M.C.A. hut which has tolerably good cooks in it. Very fortunately however a kind friend has this day sended unto me a huge crate of food from Fortnum and Masons. Whereby hangs a sad tale, In my enthusiasm I dropped a pot of jam which cracked rather badly. Refusing to waste any and disregarding the instructions given me in my youth by a wise mother, I tipped it into another pot and took it to tea. The result will doubtless prove fatal. Lady, I ate a <u>huge</u> piece of glass and cut almost the whole of my mouth away. Terrible, and me so young. I have since disposed of the jam, so don't write and tell me to.

I assume you have had a lot of skating and tobogganing – lucky devils. I skated twice, once at home when on leave (what ages ago that seems!) and once on Devizes pond. This last was a riot. Being dressed as a soldier (N.B. I refuse to say "being a soldier"!) all the myriad little kids clambered round me and called me "soldier" which always makes me feel a bit of a fool as I never know how a "soldier" is meant to react to these various occasions. Well anyhow I tried to be hearty which I find very hard at any time and eventually escaped and mucked around quite happily until these kids suddenly decided they'd like me to pull them along on the ice. They kept getting in my way and screaming so screechily that I couldn't bear it any longer and gave one of them a pull. Immediately the whole child population of Devizes turned out and demanded to be pulled. It was awful. One cunning girl aged 8 kept throwing pseudo fainting fits in a precocious attempt to gain the male interest but after she had complained that she had put out her knee, (giving local colour to her act by the most horrible screams) and so induced me to tow her to the side of the pond, she walked off quite easily and so man was once more deceived. The afternoon ended by my having to rescue a ridiculous dog which had fallen in and was unable to get out again, during the course of which I got extremely wet and was periodically asked by the horrible children whether I knew that my trousers were all wet. Grrr.

When on leave I was pretty well behaved and did nothing too violent or outrageous. I went to one very dull party but for the most part enjoyed myself by being extremely lazy. I was up in London when the whole city was set ablaze that Sunday night and several incendiaries fell through the glass roof of Waterloo Station just ahead of me. It was really rather a fine view though it made you sick with anger at the futility of it all. I had to walk from Waterloo at midnight to Paddington where I arrived abut

2.30 having spent about ¾ hour looking for the house where I was now meant to be passing the night. On finding the house I discovered it consisted of 4 flats with (naturally!) 4 doorbells. I took a malicious joy in thinking that if I rang the wrong one a complete stranger would be aroused from his bed at 2.30 all to no purpose, and rang the top one. It happened however to be the right one. That was the only excitement I had. By the way hitchhiked home from there with huge success, arriving at Piccadilly Circus at 4.15. I left the Barracks at 1.30 and a car stopped which took me all the way to London and gave me tea on the way. Pretty lucky, huh?

I like "All the Things you are" but loathe "Until You Fall in Love"!! I really had no idea you were such a poetess – how do you do it? Or does the moon shine so very brightly in bonnie Scotland? My middle name is Cleotpre nasty pronounced Michael and my birthday is on July 9th. What more can I tell you? (always excluding what you're like! Don't forget I've only seen you for something under 24 hours!)

Finally my quotation. Really Mhairi thou shouldst know your own Rabbie Burrns. Fare thee weel my best and fairest, fare thee weel my best and dearest" or maybe it's the other way round. Anyway it doesn't really matter much.

Do forgive me for being so late in replying and I am so glad to find you're mad. – with love John

[R.I.P. my socks!!!]

7 Feb

939010 Cadet J C Butler
125th O.C.T.U. RA
Fernhill
Skipton Road
Ilkley
YORKS

My dear Mhairi,

I presume that you have long ago abandoned hope of hearing from me. As you see I am at Ilkey at an O.C.T.U. and we all walk around the Moor without a hat before breakfast, haha very funny indeed and terribly original.

We've been here just over a week, having left Devizes on Wednesday 29th Jan and travelled all through the night – a wearisome process, we changed at every other station at hours forsaken of the deity, such as 3 a.m. etc. etc. etc. and had to walk from station to station and platform to platform carrying all our possessions, not to mention full equipment (very full) and 4 blankets and I had a sleeping bag, a case and a very heavy kit bag. We walked (staggered) about 5 yards and then stopped for 5 mins rest. The intervals between trains we filled in by consuming horrible food at gloomy Y.M.C.A. canteens. Most depressing. Fortunately, however we had a wonderful shave and wash on Leeds Station. It really is the nicest station I've ever seen – all modern as we say in Yorkshire. Eventually we arrived here about 10 a.m. Thursday and signed hundreds of forms and saw hundreds of people including the Battery Commander who is a Major and who was extremely and unnecessarily rude to everyone. For the first month they seem to spend their time in this place bullying you and pounce on you for the slightest fault. The intention, I presume, being to make you tear your hair and abandon interest in being an officer. It is a 5 month course and you're liable to be picked at at any time if they don't like you. Having been here a week I have got a long way to go yet. If on the other hand I withstand the mental, spiritual, moral, psychic strain imposed I shall emerge as a 2nd Lieut somewhere about the end of June.

You've no idea how much a gunner officer has to know. In fact he is a sort of encyclopedia when he has passed 5 months here. After one week I've filled hundreds of notebooks. Very expensive. I daren't try and revise them as they make us want to be sick, which is messy. We work 7 hours a day but a few extra parades get shared in here and there just for fun and we always have to be early for everything so it ends up nearly 8.. The 1st month is excessively dull for the most part. Boring lectures and marching round and round in squares. Ugh. Later we crash about country on motorbikes and things which should be far more to the point. After Devizes this course is a bit of a change, all this work, but I think it is definitely a welcome change. Apart from work we do have quite a good time. We are addressed as "gentlemen" and treated as such which is somewhat different from the sergeants' opinion of us at Devizes! We have orderlies to make our beds and clean our stuff, and we feed in a hotel where food is excellent, cooked by

A.T.S. In the evenings we stagger down to the town for a drink. We are billeted in a large house, 46 of us. (There are about 450 cadets altogether here.) It was terribly cold but we have got fires going now in the sitting and some of the bedrooms and it is quite pleasant. In the summer I think Ilkley should be very satisfactory. At present it is clad in a mantle of slush. Don't like slush. Never have not since I was a teeny weeny baby waby. I suppose you're snow bound too. How's life with you? I have no doubt that school is as romantic, as novel and as thrilling as ever, n'est ce pas? I am going rapidly to sleep owing to the proximity of large fire and enormous weight of food in stomachs. We went out to tea and rapidly (everything has to be done rapidly in this place) demolished 5 cakes apiece, not to mention toasted teacakes. I do love eating and I do love eating nice cakes. The shops here are really are very good indeed.

I should adore some spiral socks and I'm sure the Home Guard could use them in case of – shall we say accidents? (That's a cruel one, babe, huh?) Really it is very charming of you to make these offers. I'm sure you must regret them pretty soon after you've made them, but it shows you must have a nice mind, which is so important in a young (haha young) girl, don't you find, my dear contemporary? Your letter is upstairs and I can't be bothered to go and fetch it as I am half asleep. So I shall probably fail to answer something you specially asked. On 2nd thought's I don't think I ought to burden you with task of knitting socks. 12 is a bit much and I'm sure you're so busy. We get no leave from this place, except for a long weekend which is quite useless anyway. Silly, isn't it? I am endeavouring to remember a nice friend with tons of money who lives near

Ilkley I am failing to do so. Again I say "Silly, isn't it?" The people here seem quite nice on the whole though of course I don't know them at all well yet. Wonder how I'll feel after 5 months. 5 months! What an appalling thought.

Well s'long pal and behave yoursel' in a seemly way,

    Love
     John

March 2ⁿᵈ   Fernhill
                                    Skipton Road
                                    Ilkley

My dear Mhairi,

Whoopee! I feel fine today. I feel fine yesterday I feel fine tomorrow. On Friday we had our first month's exam and on Friday we had the Colonel's inspection and on Friday we gave lecturettes on M.T. (Motor Transport that means in case your poor feminine brain is ignorant thereof).

Tis this exam that is the very devil, Mhairi. Everybody who has been here for over a month says "Oh the first Month's exam is terribly important. You stand or fall by that exam." Now it is over we're being told that actually it's the 2ⁿᵈ month which counts! C'est la vie. This was the exam which kept us all in for a fortnight with our noses to our books. This was the exam which filled us with evil forebodings and led to the most colourful language on the part of everybody. Now it is over of course we be wondering why we ever did so much work as all the questions were about things we'd hardly thought of, and the things we had specially prepared we never got. C'est la vie. The Colonel's inspection was just as bad. We all dressed as would a woman going to a ball and hardly dare move for fear of disarranging our trousers. I now have an insight into the agony which your charming sex must feel when setting out for a dance or some such, lest a vital string etc. should break!

We were told that we were a smart looking troop, but our boots were not good enough, gentlemen. It is now eventide and I have had a most unsatisfactory supper of very badly disguised tinned meat. They gave it a sort of jacket of batter, but it was quite obvious what it was. We spent the afternoon lying under filthy motor trucks. I had to inspect the water cooling system. There was a leak. I had to find out where it was. I lay on my back beneath the truck, my head stuck in a patch of grease left by some careless comrade, while water dripped slowly and deliberately from the leak. This did not facilitate the task of finding the said leak. I have had a bath but haven't begun to get the oil petrol grease dirt etc. etc. etc. etc off.

I do envy you your poetic walk! I definitely have premonitions of Spring but my area is the parade ground and not the heather. I will not grieve too much when the war is over, and I shall prefer I think the heather to the parade ground.

We have a long week-end fairly soon and I think I shall go home though I shall only get a day and a half there. It would, I think, be rather pleasant, is it not so.

I feel I must congratulate you prematurely on your 5 bonny boys and the oyster satin, and even, with tears n my eyes, of the withered flowers. I guess you are within sight of the end of term, big girl! Lucky Mhairi, you will be able to rush around the countryside in ever increasing circles and getting a huge appetite. When shall we see our dear Cambridge again? Perhaps I'll meet you up there some day, huh!

Well, must end

With much love John

391.98 Field Regt RA
C/o 9po
Bembridge I.O.W.

Saturday March 21st 1941

Well, little girl, and how's yersel? What a long time since I saw you and how nasty the weather is. I have moved into residence as see in the Isle of Wight. Before the war we used to go a lot to Yarmouth. This, sweet ignoramus, is in the west of the island. Bembridge is right in the east. In consequence I know the east end but ill while I know the west end much better. Yarmouth is the most lovely place. A tiny little place with a harbor and a lifeboat and an old castle on the quay. We used to stay at the King's Head and I remember Daddy going of the deep end because beer had been raised from 6d to 7d a pint when we were there. In those days Daddy used to have his pint of bitter while I had a pint of ginger beer. I doubt very much if I could stomach a pint of ginger beer now.

We knew the harbour master and the old loafers very well and had a lot of fun. It's one of the most peaceful spots I know. I mean was – doubtless it is now seething with licentious soldiery. I must go over on the old motorbike and have a look at it. The downs by Freshwater provide a delightful ramble for visitors. A luverly view of the horizon may be had from

Tennyson's Monument and teas may be bought from the Bull and Bush Hotel in Freshwater itself. Oh god I'm a fool. We had some great holidays there just mucking about and sailing and bathing. Quite a pre-war type of holiday in fact. You know, Vari, this country can't grow up, can it? Here we are talking a lot of drivel about sun and sand and sandwiches and seagulls and Hitler is talking a lot of sense about killing the enemy and fighting the war. We must wake up. It's the most appalling nightmare the way we go stupidly procrastinating and reminiscing. We won't live in the present and we'll get it in the neck if we don't. I am the most hopeless idiot where politics are concerned but it gives me shivers when I do stop to think.

What price Houseman:

> Oh tis dancing jesting drinking
> Spins the heavy world around
> If young hearts were not so clever
> Why, they would be young forever
> Cease to think, it's only thinking
> Lays lads underground.

You must be a little tired of having this quoted at you. I believe I do it at regular quarterly intervals and yet my sweet, I'd like to spend months with you in Scotland doing very little that you could put in a Guide Book.

Have just seen *Dangerous Moonlight* which I thought excellent – and a good tune!

As for understanding you or anyone else or even myself, I recall from my rather more cultural days that the motto over the Delphic Oracle was "know thyself." This I believe to be most dangerous advice. It's perturbing if you're suffering from a liver to discuss what horribly low motives one has for doing things.

But as for the accusation that I take a low view of women I must protest.

I love your fair sex. The idea or of woman or is extremely attractive to me. One is bound to admit that 20% are brainless, 20% are soulless, 20% too old, 20% too young, and 19% are satisfactorily married. In this island the average age appears to be 65. We are working hard. Everyone has got a mad craze for paper. Consequently we are snowed up with papers saying Do this by 1900 hours; give a return of this by 1645 hours. Consequently we are in a perpetual whirl and consequently we are all going mad. Damn it. When do you break up, petite? And how long holidays do you get?

I hope to get leave in April which means I'll get some more (maybe!) in July. So mon morceau de fluff, I will see you then – no? Ah mais oui, j'insiste. Sois gentile, ma petite maori.

I'm sure I told you our island's name. It is l'Ile aux Moins. The Monks' Island. Oh come on, cough up a photograph.

Christmas comes but once a year and you did promise. And as for school being the best part of your life – phooey. It just ain't so.

Mhairi darling, this war is serious and this country of ours must wake up and realize it. Blast it anyway. Take care of yourself and be a fairly bad girl. With lots of love

John xx

Please note

Middleton Hotel
Ilkley
5th May 1942

My dear Mhairi,

I do hope you got my last letter. Since writing, we have moved from Fernhill to some curious prehistoric pygmy huts in the garden of the Middleton Hotel. Every morning we wake up to find another hut has been erected. They consist of floorboards which fail to meet at either end, leaving a 6 inch draught space directly under my bed, and of a double thickness of cardboard, the designed to give the impression of the inside of a civilized dwelling, the outer coated with tar, When the sun shines the tar melts and drops off. The next day it rains and the rain enters with much joy through the places where the tar ought to be. There is a fire in the middle of the hut. On the first day this was lit, we entered the hut and saw 8 beds, 4 each side, and a cosy hut. We said "But how too too romantic and cosy." Aren't men fools?

That piece of artistry represents Our Hut in section. Do not be misled into thinking the objects portrayed are mushrooms. They are as a matter of fact beds. On the beds you have 3 biscuits. A biscuit is a square thing filled with bricks and nails and rough edged stones. 3 biscuits are put on the springs of the bed. i.e. 3 biscuits = 1 mattress (theoretically). I need not mention that mine don't begin to fit. Consequently I have a 6 inch gap between each biscuit. Consequently the draught takes this excellent opportunity to whistle up through the gaps. I may mention that they are called biscuits because the great and glorious English Army (sorry, British Army – I was forgetting your origin!) in its laudable puerility thinks they look like biscuits. Isn't it wonderful? Look. My bed from the top

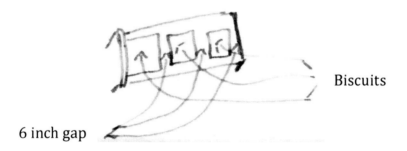

Biscuits

6 inch gap

Such is the tale I have to tell. 'Smatter of fact we rather like these huts. Saturday and Sunday were so hot we took off practically everything and sunbathed on the wee bit awn behind the hut. Twas verra pleasant.

Today again is dull, but thank God the trees and birds and things are beginning to wake up and up on the moors it's very nice, though not, I fancy, as nice as Scotland is. I suppose with this extra-extra hour it never gets dark at all up your way. Soon we'll be having the day in the night. Not a bit funny. Pardon.

When I wrote I had not seen your note saying your dog had been killed. I'm so sorry, Mhairi. You must have felt awful. Was he the famous dog that was mostly a setter, or was he a Scottie? I can't quite remember but I do remember your saying that I must meet him some time. On 3rd thoughts I'm not sure it wasn't a wire haired terrier. I must be getting old and decrepit as I used once to pride myself somewhat on my memory.

I suppose you're back at school again by now. Well, at least the summer is the best term. I always thought so, anyway, in the far far off days of long ago when I was at school, Little Girl! We finish this course (which is not at all unlike school incidentally) in about 6 weeks time. We have a weekend's leave on May: 16th which is a cheering thought.

I have a feeling my writing is probably illegible. I am really getting quite a complex about this as everybody tells me how awful it is. The point is that I always write letters in the most peculiar positions, with one leg round me neck, etc. I don't know why but it always happens that way.

They are now playing some soft and soothing music on the wireless. This wireless is the bane of my existence. It goes on when you switch on the lights in consequence thereof, when the orderlies come in about 6 a.m. to clean the boots the horrid wireless goes on with a loud snort and I am rudely awakened to hear Cookery Hints or Physical Jerks For the Over Forties or something of the sort. Such is life.

The soft sweet music has now ended and I must go and have some tea (they call it tea). I do hope you re well, and as cheerful as ever.

With much love,

John

The Three Musketeers Roy Heckscher,
Tom Davis and John Butler

Middleton Hotel
Tuesday 27th May 1941

My dear Mhairi,

What I say is, there's nothing like today and gorn tomorrow and so on. What I mean is don't you think? This is a clever way of saying I don't seem to have written for some time. The time as such is now passing pretty rapidly. We go out from this hole in 20 days. Which reminds me that it is not Tuesday 27th but Thursday 29th. Since beginning this letter (i.e. writing the address on top) we have been out on night occupation and been rushed around from one place to another pulling guns and things. It has been most awfully strenuous. We have also had to give lecturettes on gunnery subjects. They give you 20 mins to prepare same. The Colonel came in during mine. Always was I lucky. However I knew a little about it and he obviously didn't know anything at all, so I was all right. We are now faced with the prospect of Final Exams, on Sat the day after tomorrow. There is so much to do that I have done nothing. You see there is so much I don't know where to start, so if I never start I cannot ever learn anything. See? You will notice from the style of my letter that I am going mad. After a man on the wireless has just started to sing a curious song called "Strong is my Creed". Very disturbing – tends to distract. It is 1 o'clock and it is of course raining. It has been raining for as long as I can remember in Ilkley, though at last the trees are out and so are the bluebells.

Ilkley has just realized that spring is practically over, and is trying to make up for lost time. In 10 mins I have to see the colonel. Hell. Am consulting my watch. I find it is ten past two. Alas, I fly. Farewell. I am now back. It is almost tea-time. The Colonel was very pleasant. I may well be going in the Surrey Yeomanry which my Papa was in once upon a time before the war. This is only surmise. In fact I may go almost anywhere I guess. What matter? Don't you think soon we shall have a show-down as the American films would say? Us versus Hitler. I meant to apologise for the paper some time ago. It is really the paper I do rough work on (when I do rough work) and is no sort of paper to write to a fair young maiden on. But knowing your large and generous heart I feel confident you will readily forgive me.

The school with which I decorated my presence and (or vice versa) was Aldenham, in answer to your kind enquiry, dear madam. Further in response to yours of the somethingth inst. I didn't go home for the weekend (and how dare you suggest we have an awful lot of weekends, psha ugh! lady) but walked in the Lake District – lovey it were. Quite 'ot and very peaceful.

The tune you quote –The London I love – sounds most heart wringing and I feel that if I were to hear it, apart from reminding me at once of your beautiful self, I should almost certainly burst into tears. Actually the only tune I ever seem to hear is called The First Lullaby, and nobody has yet explained to me what exactly "The echo of a lonely sigh" is. J'attendrai. Of course I know well; nice tune but murdered by the horrible Tino Rossi who usually sings it. Nothing like a little destructive criticism! As you say, I am marvelous at cricket. I have played in 17 Test Matches all under different names.

Finally I grieve over Tiggy's moustache and will pray that another may quickly grow.

Au revoir, wee lassie,

Wi luve John

3/7/41

98th7d Regt RA
Fort Southwick
Fareham
HANTS

My dear, dear Mhairi,

How I have the sauce, nay the restraint rather, to abstain from writing to you for such an interval I just cannot understand. I am now a 2nd Lieutenant. The wireless is spouting news at a distance of one foot six from my right ear. No wonder I cannot think straight. Probably I shall write like this – I mean the Germans the Russians say that in a recent battle the spokesman of Benkavina girls no official confirmation of the German assertion that the Black Sea has been shot down. If you see what I mean. Really your last letter was utterly delightful and charming. I'm so glad you enjoyed Hamish's wedding. I imagine you must have looked simply ravishing. If only I could have been there to walk out of the church with you, as I did so gracefully before. Surely you remember? Oh how can you. You are a one, you are. Cor yes. I am going potty on account of this wireless. I am just unable concentrate one jot or tittle. It is too much for my futile brain. The talking-box has now ceased its idle chatter. Around me my jovial companions play at poker. Last night I played at poker and was losing an incredible amount of money until the last ten minutes when I redeemed myself and my exchequer. See the temptations in the path of an innocent and credulous young man. I am completely at sea in this place. Tomorrow I have to deliver a lecture to the officers and also have a thorough inspection of the workings of a truck about which I know absolutely nothing. As days go on I see myself as the very lowest of the low, subalterns, doing the most irksome and unpleasant duties Life assumes horrifying possibilities. This is a crack regiment. It does everything at the run and it spends an enormous proportion of time blancoing belts and cleaning brass. It is really no place at all for me. There are already far too many officers in this place – all subalterns nearly. Eh bien, c'est la vie, as we used to say in the good old days (tears are streaming down my face).

As for past history, I left Ilkley on Wednesday June 18th. We ended our cadetship with an orgy of parties and I felt quite worn out and ready for 7 days leave. It was marvelous at home. I did absolutely nothing except loaf about on the river all day long. Glorious. The weather was crackerjack or superb or very good indeed, Miss, thank you. Mr and Mrs Kil are well and I had a drink with Tig who was just finishing his 7 days. It was good to see him again, and we won the war together in about half an hour. Mr Kil made some charming remarks about you as you can readily imagine, and all of which you merit (roser!). On June 26th I went to Larkhill where we had a lot of fun firing the guns at real targets. Such a thrill. We finished the course early so I got another 2 days leave before coming down here on July 1st. The weather has been very kind, but it's no joke having to put on their stuff in the heat, after having spent my leave in a shirt and pair of trousers. I therefore trust that sometime within the next ten years this war will end as slacks suit me better than khaki I have decided, as far as comfort is concerned.

I enjoyed your horticulture immensely. It made my mouth water – "Oh the bonny braes and doons". Furthermore I shall never be able quite to express the enormous debt I owe you for having explained to me the echo of a lonely sigh. Oh kind and clever poetess!

So you are sure I am lazy, are you? Never a truer word. I am the personification of laziness and am quite brown from sunbathing. This army life is far too energetic really. Still they feed us quite well. Which is something, n'est ce pas? I shall have now to end this epistle I'm afraid in order to drag myself to bed. Then I sleep and then I get up again to face another day, and eat and work and sleep again. Would you explain to me, please, the reason we exist? You're so <u>good</u> at explaining, Vari dear.

With love

Jhohum (force of habit!)

Oh don't forget to give Sue my love, will you

13/7/41

98th Field Regt RA
Fort Southwick
Fareham
HANTS

Mhairi dear,

You are quite certainly the nicest girl I know and your letters are sweet. Thank you so much for writing and thank you so much for drinking my health. I drank yours, with trembling hands, a full heart and an empty stomach, in sherry. Not very good sherry, not as good as the champagne that you and I will drink together when the war is won, my rred rred rrose. And thank you so much for your present. I haven't got it yet but my faith is absolute. You must take me to Craighill very soon and we'll pick all the gooseberries and eat all the rasberries and strip all the orchards. And we'll go on the lake by moonlight and picnic on the edge. And we'll dance a reel in the village street. And I shall beat you at billiards and you'll beat me up at croquet because I should never have the heart to knock your ball or bowl (or whatever sort of sphere it is that you use in this spiteful game) away from the hoop. And as for the heather – oh Mhairi, we'll walk for miles together dot dot dot dot dot dot dot dot dot dot. And here am I stuck in Hampshire where it's hot and sticky and sometimes it pours with rain and everything gets covered in mud and has to be cleaned. See, I can be almost as sentimental as you, wee lassie! Will you thank Sue once more for her kind thought and wishes. I should like to meet her too. You must be a charming couple. Tell her that I will certainly heed her warning – you wouldn't doubt it? – and be a very good little boy. If I am given a key it will be a great help. At home I always used to lose mine, and climb up the drainpipe into my bedroom window. You had to be awfully sober.

I hope, by the way, that you have since had my letter. I believe I wrote about a week ago. I had been pretty busy actually, and it was nice of you to say so. I didn't write when I was home on leave as I didn't know the address I should be coming to. You ask what sort of thing to give to men! Well, well, well Miss Falconer. 20 1/2 and you haven't found out that yet! To be perfectly honest I never know what I want; I mean I always want a 1930 Bentley and a yacht or two and a thousand pounds and possibly a small aeroplane, but people are so awkward about giving you that sort of present nowadays. I don't know why. However I had the following: a wristwatch, a Revelation suitcase, Beethoven's 5th Symphony, books, photograph albums, cigarette lighter and some money. If I can rouse my younger sister I may get a present out of her too!

I had a very quiet day on my birthday, funnily enough. The night before I went out and had a party and when endeavoring to return on a borrowed motorbike about midnight or so, the damned thing conked out half way home and when I had exhausted my supply of language upon it, I had to take it to a garage and walk 4 miles home uphill. And I wasn't really in any condition for walking 4 miles home uphill. So that is why I spent a quiet day on Wednesday! But I did eat a large bowl of salad and fruit salad, as there were only 2 of us in to dinner. And I did toast you, Mhairi, most deeply.

There are so many things we must do when the war is finished. When we've spent the summer at Craighill (see page 1!) you'll come down to London and we'll go out to dinner and the theatre, rushing through the lighter streets of Town in a taxi because we are slightly late after the theatre we'll go and dance till morning. Then we'll think at how we can spend the new day. And if the war ends within ten years or so and I go back to Cambridge you must come to the May Ball and we'll have breakfast up the river in a punt. Oh there are so many things to be done. Won't someone put a knife in Hitler's liver?

I have talked enough drivel. I shall thank you once again, and once again say how charming I think you are – big girl!

Take care of yourself,
With lots of love JOHN

P.S. Excuse pencil Hope you can read this.

26/7/41 98ᵗʰ Field Regt RA
Fort Southwick
Fareham
Hants

Ma chere Vari,

I have undergone a tragedy. I begin, il y a trois jours, to write and thank you for your so nice present. And damn it if I didn't lose the letter. I left my writing pad with the letter in it and now both are gone. So some swine has not only pinched my notepaper, but probably read my letter as well. And doubtless the beauty, nay sublimity, of it, was lost upon his meager soul. So now after receiving your most kind and delightful letter this morning, I hasten to write once more and say how sweet of you it was to send me AEH. Did you know I had gone crazy on Housman? I said I had infinite trust in your taste and powers of choice. It was a lovely present; thank you so much. You must thank Sue for me if and when you write to her. Thank her for her good wishes, congratulations felicitations etc. and also for drinking my health in Vimto. Was it Vimto? Some day she must drink champagne with us!

I was quite amazed to see a Paddington postmark on your letter. I hope you enjoy Swansea. I don't think myself I'd leave the Highlands for Swansea, no, not no how. But I hope you don't get rained on either with rain or bombs. Rain seems more in the fashion now. While I am cheerfully writing to Swansea, I am forgetting that perhaps you did get lost in London and are even now running round on all fours gasping madly and grunting with hunger and rage. I do hope not.

It's sad about Tiggy[4]. Sheila won't like it much I don't expect. Personally I wouldn't mind swapping places as long as I knew I was coming back fairly soon! I am getting a little tired of these drat red walls that surround us on every side. But then I am not burdened with a wife! Nothing like a little freedom. Anyhow I hope old Tig. Comes back pretty soon. We'll all be glad to see him.

In about five minutes I have got to elevate myself from this chair and go and mount the guard. As it is the first time I have ever mounted the guard I shall probably do the most amazing things. Also it is raining, which is another reason why I am unwilling to vacate this comparatively comfortable chair. Furthermore, we have to go get up at 3 o'clock tomorrow morning (Sunday) in order to go on some horrrible scheme. Last Sunday was also spent on a scheme. Next Sunday we're not allowed to travel because of crowding the railway . C'est la vie, alors! I have now turned, I mean returned, from mounting the guard which I did with amazing success. Most amazing. I've been having an awful time. I told you that last weekend we went on what the newspapers call "large scale exercises". Well during the course of 2 ½ days, I, the most junior and newly arrived subaltern in the regiment, succeeded in a) losing two guns and

---

[4] to Burma

several food lorries b) in crashing a motorcycle and c) in nearly ruining the whole scheme by stopping the guns in entirely the wrong place, thereby preventing all other traffic from using said road. Wasn't it frightfully funny. You'd never believe 6 ft odd could feel so small. We had a huge night journey. Rain and no moon or stars and no lights at all on vehicles. Well first of all in rounding up the convoy on my motorbike I got left miles behind and shooting along a straight road at 35 mph in pitch dark, the road chose that moment to cease being straight and turn itself into a corner. Well I naturally went straight on. I went absolutely slap into the ditch, the bike stopped very suddenly (not unnaturally) and I went over the handlebars. The bike then landed on top of me from a great height. Stars swam pleasantly in front of my eyes. Being, as you know, of a philosophic turn of mind, I said: "Oh well I'm dead. It's quite pleasant." After a time I became sadly disillusioned and found I was alive and dripping with blood. Having conquered an urge to bleed quietly to death, I thought I'd better have a look at the bike. The bike was a peculiar shape. Headlamp hanging buy the flex, handlebars at an unusual angel, mudguard buckled. So much I took in at a glanced. I daren't look for anything else. I thought I'd better try and start it, just for the principle of the thing. I thought it'll probably blow up, but instead it started. Amazing. I rode it with the handlebars in the region of my head and the mudguard scraping the wheel, for some thousands of miles. Then by an amazing piece of mapreading I caught up with the convoy. I got a hammer and hammered the bike into approximately the right shape. It was about 2.30 a.m., and I haven't been so cold for years and years. I got in the back of a private car and went to sleep. I believe you get shot for doing this on active service.

When I woke up the convoy had moved and I knew not whither. Hence point c) mentioned above. What a life. Ever since I have been reminded of these things by everybody from the Colonel downwards. Och lassie, what a life it is.

I'm glad you agreed with the sentiments expressed in my lyrical outburst. I always knew you were a nice girl? Wouldn't it be fun if we could meet somewhere. Haha. But somehow I think it's one of those things that don't happen. I have a feeling it will be in either London or Edinburgh that we shall see each other.

I have become signals officer in the Troop. What I know of signaling would go in a thimble with plenty of room to spare. So I insisted on having a class of gunners and drivers who know even less. Nevertheless some of them are dangerously intelligent and ask the most embarrassing questions. Today I lectured them on elementary electricity. Laugh. Young lady, do you know how an electric bell works? Or do you confine your researches to the meaning of lonely sighs and mens' existence? You know child, for 13 ¾ years you are very wise. Quite a promising kid. Signed Methusaleh. What I mean is your explanation of existence. It is absolutely masterly. Remind me when I do see you to wipe my feet on your person.

The troop I am in, to wit A Troop, is always working. Everybody else has half holidays and things but not A Troop. We came back from a scheme at 3 in the morning and start right away cleaning the guns. The latest joke amongst A Troop now is that when the war is over the whole Regiment of Royal

Artillery will be lined up and the King will say: Royal Regiment of Artillery dismiss: A Troop stand fast." Haha. Very funny that.

Tonight I shall ring up home. In fact I will go and do so right away. It usually takes 3 hours as far as I can gather. I am thinking of buying a motorbike. Since my meeting with the ditch however my interest in motorbikes has considerably decreased.

Well, Mhairi dhear, I must bid you a fond farewell and once more thank you for your lovely present and all your charming letters. Do please write some more when you feel so inclined.

With love John

17/8/41   98th7d Regt RA
                                     RAPC Mess
                                     Larkhill
                                     Salisbury Plain

Well my dear Vari,

I havna written to you for a long time noo it seems. In fact a century, an age, an aeon. It is not so? As you see we have moved to Larkhill. Isn't it perfectly foul? I don't know if you know anything about Larkhill but if you don't, keep your pure and unspoilt young soul untainted with the noisome place. It is covered with tin huts and is a horrible mass of barracks and soldiers. Soldiers teem. Even Salisbury is devoid of civilians. Oh it's a poisonous spot. I have never spent more than 3 days before. That was ample. The mercury that is my spirit, sank to its lowest ebb. We moved here on Friday. We shall probably stay here for 8 months. Grrr. It's horrid.

Thank you for the heather which we call ling in the sophisticated South. Actually down Portsmouth way the real heather is out. Why won't they send us to Scotland? Larkhill of all places in England. Someone shall suffer for this. Beware. Signed the Red Horrrror. The someone will be us, I refuse to discuss it any more. Let's talk about you. How's the Y.M.C.A? Do the soldiers whistle and wink and leer at you as soldiers should? And have you bought your cottage yet? I have only passed once through Swansea and I think I thought it was Cardiff or versi vica if you understand my meaning. I didn't think it was at all nice in any case. Your idyllic cottage and your paradisal bathe seems to belie my impression. Is Cuthbert still aloft, or has he been blasted by thundering Jupiter and sent crashing to the earth in a ball of flame? Poor Cuthbert, I do hope not. It sounds perfectly horrid. I must apply for a curse in Scotland I think. I should really love to see you. I cant' really recall what you look like, but you always seemed to be laughing. Heigh ho!

Love, John

25/9/41

The Haven
West Parade
Rhyl, N Wales

Dear Mhairry

You will curse me, if you are so unladylike, for not having written to you for so long. I am as you perceive immediately with your magnificent mind, in North Wales, We have been here almost a fortnight now. It's rather good fun. It is an M.T. Course that I am here on and it lasts a month at the end of which I return to the ghastly Larkhill. We work quite amazingly hard, doing 8 ½ hours work a day. The weekends however we are given free from 11.30 on Saturday. The idea of the course it to learn all about vehicles and motorbikes. We drive them and pick them to pieces and have lectures on them. The lecture part is dull but the rest is rather good fun. Next week we are on motorbike and climb mountains and ride through rivers and things. So far the weather has been superb and it has been generally been very pleasant. You will by now be back at school is it not? And what a big girl! My dear, I remember you when you were sprawling on a rug gurgling. We have been out all day driving and having to repair things and fit chains and spare wheels and things and I am more than ½ asleep, so forgive me if this letter is extremement dull. Did you go to Craighill, and was it all it should be? McKil said something about going to Scotland when I saw him but I can't remember what. I hope you see him if he does. He really could do with a holiday – or so my parents say, he always looks the picture of health to me. However I maintain that everybody works and feels a lot better for a holiday.

Hamish seems to have had a tough time – I didn't hear him on the wireless, no doubt as I was working at the time. Work. We are always working. Tiggy I gather has now actually gone abroad and Sheila is joining the Wrens? One day, ma petite, when the war is in its fortieth year, you too will be becoming a landgirl or something. This war really does want to be speeded up or our unfortunate descendants will have to learn about the 100 years war. I am now getting vaguer and vaguer. We are going to see the Marx Bros Go West tonight. They always make me laugh like a row of crickets, which probably betrays softheadedness on my part. I shall go to sleep.

We are waited on at lunch by a horde of queer ATS. Why are ATS always queer? Rhyl is full of queer people – it is a typical seaside resort – hundreds of boarding houses, a pier, pavilion, dance hall, souvenir shops and fun fair and things. And only about half the population wear khaki which is a change form Larkhill where they all do. I have however the cheering thought of 7 days leave about October 23rd. Just about October 23rd. What is there about October 23rd? Would you like a sturgeon or a very small alligator? Yoo ya oolga nor I have gone potty. All replies to The Haven, The Asylum or the Loony Bin if you please. I have now fallen off into a fitful sleep. Sleep that knits up the unravelled sleeve of care. There are quite a nice lot of blokes up here which is satisfactory, but the food is not all satisfactory really, being not plentiful, or scarce as you might say. Meat roll keeps appearing in different forms from day to day and meal to meal.

If you put pen to paper and send to me a missive, I will be here until October 9\th and then at Larkhill where my address in case you have lost it, is 391/98\th Field Regt RA Larkhill, Wilts. I shall be intrigued to hear how you spent your holiday, how you feel, how school is (I bet you're bored) and how Scotland is. Do forgive me for the dullness (correct spelling, no?) of this epistle.

With much love

John

Oct 9th/41

The Haven
West Parade
Rhyl, N Wales

Dearest one,

Thank you for your charming letter. Really it is difficult to concentrate. The wireless is playing the most filthy nonsense imaginable, my God it's awful. Outside it's raining cats and dogs which is awful too. Tonight at 8 we have got to go out on a night drive until 10. That is terrible. But our course ends on Saturday and back I go to stinking Larkshill which is the most ghastly thing of all. I have enjoyed this month enormously. I've spent pounds and pounds, drunk lots of beer, had a terrific time riding up and down mountains on a motorbike and even danced which is a thing I avoid at all costs as a general rule, out of consideration for my partner's feet.

But I hasten to express my humble congratulations. What the hell has gone wrong with Och. That you are captain of a House? It's amazing, stupendous, scintillating. That'll sober you up a bit, my child. Any advice you want old girl, just write to me and for a small (very small in the case of charming young ladies) I will pour out to you the wisdom of my years and the fruits of my experience. By the way embarrassing has two rrs in it. If a Scots has only put one & its's pretty bad – what would an English girl do? The answer is put none at all. For a 6th Former that's pretty poor. Consider yourself stood in a corner, smacked, and sent to bed without any jam for tea.

I'm interested to hear that in just a year you'll be free to do whatever you like, and even more interested to know what you'll do. It all sounds very sinister. I have just had tea. There was no jam – not good. You know, I have so many letters I ought to write and yet I somehow cannot bring myself to do any of them. Today for instance we have been winching huge tractors up mountains which involves the most awful exertions of one sort or another – it would be idle to attempt an explanation to your womanly and untutored mind – and to add to our enjoyment it poured with rain the whole time and the wind was thick about us. Consequently I feel a complete wreck and my chief desire, having eaten a large if uninspiring lunch, was to sleep. But no, we have to turn up at the garage at 2 o'clock and off we go again. Grrr.

The number of times I fell off my motorbike is difficult to calculate as I can only count up to 50 – did you know that? So yes I am a little mad – on my mother's side I think, though all my father's forbears had to be put quietly away. I am a mass of bruises and cuts and holes, but would not now hesitate to ride a bike straight up the side of a house if asked nicely by a pretty girl, being as you may know, frightfully susceptible to female charm. Did you know that?

Your request for an island shall, I think, be granted, but we must await the cessation of hostilities, as the island concerned is French. It lies off the South Coast of Brittany and is the most romantic place on earth. It shall be thine for the writing of perfect poetry and noble novels. Lambkins abound and the turtledove grows on every bush. My dear, it's too too glamorous for verbal utterance. Oh dear it is going to be wet tonight, and I had hoped for a moon which would make the night driving so much easier. Even you can understand that. What do you look like nowadays – have you changed very much in word or deed? And did you go to Craighill and what do you know?

I shall now terminate this epistle in order to get some of my things together before Saturday as I feel that if I don't do it now I never shall. So I will wish you, honey, the best of luck in controlling all your horrid little girls, - kmost little girls are horrid aren't they? And I wish you well. If you should deign to write you have my Larkhill address I think, - otherwise send it home. Just please yourself little cabbage –

With love John

391/98 7d Regt RA
RA PC Mess
Larkhill
Wiltshire

Oct 17th 1941

Ah my beloved, for your letter so many thanks; for the sentiments expressed words cannot tell – I give my heart. It will arrive later by parcel post – being of enormous dimensions it will not fit into a letter box. Is it to be a year before I stand face to face with you, is it 360 days before I hear the music of your laugh, before I see the pearl of your smile and the sparkle of your eyes. No, no, time you old laggard. Run.

"Ocelerruie currite, noctus equi"
I cannot bear it. The seasons change, the earth moves round the sun, time passes that shall not return, Jack has Jill, the sauce has its pan, the collar has its stud, the ink has its pot. But I have you not. Send me some horrible photos of your exquisite self – it is the least you can do – oh I cannot bear it. I faint – I have a drink of water – I feel fine thanks. How are you.

So much for page 1. I am, you see, potty. And why? Ah Ladye, fayre ladye, searrrch your own heart, look in your own mirror and know why I am faint. I have had another stiff water and feel much better. At the age of 17 you are to be thrown on the hospitality of wicked London. In a year so many things can happen, but if they don't I will be ever at hand to defend you against the slings and arrows of outrageous fortune. (That's a fine ambiguous statement.) Listen, sweetheart, I am endeavouring to procure for you a birthday present but am being baulked. So will you accept my apologies, my best wishes and my love until the more concrete gift arrives. I do hope you have a happy birthday. I imagine the crowds of happy girls rushing round their beloved House Captain and cheering madly – like hell.

The 9 o'clock news is blaring forth and upsetting my train of thought.

So much for page two. Let me answer the allegations in your letter.

i) I am not dancing
ii) I am sitting in Larkhill swearing at all mankind.
iii) I have not and shall not forget our date for theatre, dinner or dance.
iv) I can boil and fry an egg (if you give me an egg), grill a steak, fry sausages, make coconut ice, and make toffee.
v) I adore omelettes, especially at two o'clock in the morning made by you
vi) How did you know I was a small and idiotic schoolboy
vii) How perfectly sweet of you to think I was reserved to females. And how perfectly true.

viii) Listen, darling. The island is shaped like a cross. It is 3 miles long and 1 ½ miles across. There are 3 woods of pine trees that stretch down to the sea – le Bois d'Amour. Le Bois de Soupirs, and le Bois de Regrets. The sea is perfectly blue and the sun shines in a blue cloudless sky. Nestling over the island, by the woods, are whitewashed gleaming cottages. The roads are dusty tracks along which peasants in national dress lazily drive dreaming cows. There is an old broken mill on the summit of the island where you can sit and watch the whole island and the little boats that sail around it – fishing boats with white and yellow and red and blue sails. There are no cars or motorbikes on the island – only one horse and two or three bicycles. There's no need because no one is in a hurry. There is a church with a clock and a tiny graveyard. And lots of little sandy bays around the coast where you can bathe and lay all day in the sun and nobody ever comes near to disturb you. There is a café where the island folk all go at night and sing old Breton songs and drink wine and eat oysters. Blackberries and figs and bilberries and apples and pears and plums grow anywhere – you may eat what you like – no property is private there.

The moon shines all night on a phosphorescent sea. It is always warm and the birds always sing in the island.

It's a nice place – there's lots more about it!

.

ix)   You wrong me, madam. I drove nothing but an army lorry in the moon light. Cross my heart. Not my fault – I hadn't got a car!
x)   I insist on having a nice photo of you of a reasonable size.
xi)   I will come to Craighill with you some day.
xii) Do you really know more than I think?
xiii) I look even more handsome than I used to (don't bother to tell me you thought it impossible) and have just refused a fourth offer from Hollywood.
xiv) Larkhill is as bad as ever.
xv)   My opinion of the no such why is here out of to for
xvi) I see I must come to Crieff to meet your matron. I can hardly wait.

I am going on leave on Thursday next and I must say I shall welcome it.

Vari dear, many happy returns – excuse the lateness of my present –

De tout mon amour,

John

Oct: 27th 1941

My dear Vari,

At long last. I hope a) you haven't got and b) you like this book. It is really an essential thing to possess.

I trust, modom, you had an appy birfday and fousands of presents.

Knowing your understanding heart, I think you will forgive the brevity of this letter – I am on leave, hurrah, and at home, hurrah and I'm just going out. Hurrah.

With beaucoup d'amour

Jean

It now appears to be Tuesday afternoon. Time verily fleeth sometimes. We have now been told the result of the exam. For some queer reason everybody seems to have got 70% or thereabouts except for one poor unfortunate who got 29% and has been slung out.

SALISBURY PLAIN
Nov 9·ᵀᴴ 1941

Well, my dear Mhairi my dear, thank you very much for your volume, thank you. It was a sweet letter you wrote and I do beg of you to write again an equally sweet and equally long letter. Presumptuous young subaltern – but I ask on behalf of N Gale Esq.[5], the singer of Berkeley Square. I think some day you must sing for me. "I have heard the mermaids singing each to each. I do not think that they will sing to me."

Now brilliant young lady, where does that one come from, huh?

Think you read poetry very beautifully and I'm awfully glad you liked the weekend Book. I think it is quite essential for every nice person to possess it and as we are both nice people and I have got a copy it follows that you should have a copy too.

I am very grieved to hear you are bedridden (lovely word!) and trust that you are by now able to take a few cautious steps across the bedroom. I hate to think of your active body and volatile spirit being caged in a bedroom, and I can't bear to

---

[5] "A Nightingale Sang in Berkeley Square" – our song very popular in 1940

think of the chaos that must reign in your House now its guide and inspiration is indisposed.

You are very rude about my heart – it is not heavy. Not since I met you (damn clever that!)

I must congratulate you on your knowledge of Doctor Faustus. Witty as well as pretty.

Oh thou art fairer than the evening air,
Clad in the beauty of a thousand stars.

But wait, art thou so fair? Art thou so charming? Art thou not fickle? Art thou not false and wicked and base and evil?

Woman, do you dare refuse me your photographic image. Nay, I will not abide it. I will take a train and get me to Ochtertyre again and I shall put you oer my knee and spank you well and heartily. What a man (you say with quickened pulse and maiden flutterings.)

I insist absolutely that you send me a nice photograph. Darling please. Now that brings me to another point. Have I really never called you darling, deliciae, in all these weary months. Oh nympha Formosa, o puella carissima! Why we are practically married. Indeed would have been had you not failed to keep tryst – you were always a bit vague about procedure in church weren't you – heaven knows why I have any more to do with you. Darling.

Now I want to know what and from what sauces I mean sources you imagine you heard about me and my island. This curiosity is natural and justifiable as you will admit with your unbiased female mind (like hell) and should make pretty fruity reading judging by your lurid imagination. I can't really tell you an awful lot more about it – at least I won't – just moonlight and stars, night and the woods and you (quotation from - ?) Just summer idyll.

Have you read *Spears Against Us* by Cecil Roberts? You would like it, having like me a soft and sentimental mind. I shall take you there, mon amie, and show you the wind mill and the woods and the bays and the fishing boats and the cottages and the Café de l'Ocean. And you shall drink champagne with me, and swim and sail and lie in the sun and talk in the evening and sing 'aupres de ma blonde'. To preserve the harmony of the scene, I will leave the singing to you. Meanwhile, (because 'Aupres de me blonde' has too many verses) I will make you brioches and toys for your delight – at (tut tut John) Birdsong at morning and star shine at night.

It will be spring when we are there. We will get up at 7 and go out – you in a cotton frock and me in slacks and an open shirt. The sun will have risen over the eastern point of the island and the fishing boats with red and yellow and blue and white sails will be out to sea in the west. The birds will be singing and nobody will be about except the vergers going to unlock the church for early service and from inside the whitewashed cottages smoke will come in a thick stream and the old women well be preparing breakfast. We will walk down the hill in the fresh morning dawn to the quay on the north point and meet the ferry boat as it comes over from the mainland with food and the morning papers. The ferry man will say it is a nice morning and is going to be a hot day. And he will give us a paper and say the government doesn't know what the hell it's doing. We will climb up the hill and have our breakfast of hot rolls and coffee. We will wash up – you'll wash and I'll dry – and make the beds and you will think about lunch. Then we'll go to the tiny muddled little shops and buy useless things. When the sun is high at midday we'll run to a tiny deserted stretch of sand and bathe while the church bells ring – they always ring at midday – and we'll lie in the sun. After lunch we'll go sailing and take galettes for tea. And in the evening when the sun is setting we'll sail back and stroll up to the café where the fisherman will be talking oh so seriously about the misgovernment of their country. And they'll ask us what we think and we'll say we don't care a damn as long as the sun continues to shine and the birds continue to sing and they continue to go out and sail and catch their mackerel. And they will look at each other and say the mad English. And I shall say non, la belle jeune fille est l'ecossaise. We'll walk home arm in arm in the moonlight.

How's that for a programme?

I wonder if Sue has written any more letters. I think she is probably not only more talented but more legible. Anyhow it's a happy thought. I am camp orderly officer tonight and I have got to sleep in a cold cold air raid shelter and guard the camp. And my lord it is cold on Salisbury plain. sigh. I definitely do not like it, Dr Fell.

Where do the odd odes come from, tell me true.

Once more I have metaphorically to spank you, caught girl How dare you say I was disgusted at sitting on those dirty logs?[6] Come, come, it is very nice to eat peaches with a charming girl, and very nice to sit on a log with an attractive girl. I'm afraid you'll die young my dear because you are an ancient 16 (on the whole!). But please try not to. Which reminds me I really ought to see you soon in case the north of England is invaded and cut off from the south by the horrrrible hun. And now I am in the same quandary as you – I'm at the beginning of a page and can't waste it. There is a lot I could say to you. You are a very easy and a very charming person to write to. But I must go to this horrible cold and lonely couch of mind. I really hope I shall see you sometime not too far distant.

Probably you'll be sweet 17 and very flirtatious before the glad day arrives. And I shall be 22 and sober. God what an age. Remind me to see if my hair is greying at the temples. If the war is over by then we'll have lots of fun in Town and see lots of shows and drink till 7 in the morning. If the war isn't over we'll see just as many shows and drink till 7 in the morning.

Goodnight my very sweet Vari.

---

[6] At Bob's wedding reception.

39/98th 7d Regt RA
Larkhill
November 28 41

My very dear Vari,

How charming and nice you are, and what a very sweet letter you wrote me. Should you send me another would you send it home as I have hopes we may move from this Zeus forsaken hovel. If we do I am told it will be to a place where you have to pump water for a mile and then boil it before it's any use to man. But this will be a change which is we are led to believe the spice of life. In the army this olds particularly true. I'm afraid it won't be to Edinburgh or even Crieff. That really would be funny. You cannot imagine how much it would make me laugh to come and take out the House Captain. Thank Sue very kindly for her letter. Being a woman I have no doubt you read it (my sisters quite shamelessly reads all my letters if I leave them about) but if by any chance you didn't it accused you of falling into a state of hysteria cum hiccups cum heart failure on receipt of my letter. I hope you have recovered your sang-froid. I am most disturbed for your health.

Do you know I have attempted to write to you three times? This is the third. My previous efforts have petered out and seem even less interesting than this. There are times when I just cannot write letters even to people like you. I have just rung up home and reversed the charges which always seems to me a vey dirty trick. One day I shall do it to you and speak for 1 hour and 25 minutes. Laugh. When does ah see thee most beloved one. I wonder if you've read all his sonnets. They always strike me as being rather rude but doubtless it's my unpoetic mind, becoming murky and sullied by the godless army. I hope you enjoyed your confirmation. I think I'm probably an atheist and almost certainly a Sun Worshipper. Occasionally I have my doubts however. Actually I'm far too lazy to question my soul. You will know what I mean – I believe in life as it is and people as they are. I told you did I not that this would be an impossible letter. I am going to see a performance of The Barber of Seville at Garrison Theatre. Talking of which recalls to me that oddly enough when I was up at Rhyl I saw the Vic Wells do Le Lac des Cygnes in Manchester. I love all Ballet Music and Tchaikovsky is especially adept at producing pleasant times.

Answers to last week's problems

1. Night and the woods and you – not by a girl friend, not by me, but by Rupert Brooke.
2. The mermaids singing each to each. From the Love Song of Alfred J Prufrock by T.S. Eliot.
3. Galettes are lovely cakes rather like shortbread. My God it makes my eyes and mouth water at the thought.

Voila, sweetheart, le lecon est fini.

How dare you suggest I should break a plate when drying up? You have mortally offended me. 2 causes are open. 2 only. Either I kill myself tonight or you do the washing and drying up. Wouldn't it be fun alone, on an island? At times I behave like a child of 2, at other times I find myself being hardboiled. Very strange. And my dear Vari is 16 years and 1 month. I have a nasty feeling this is going to be not only short but very dull. My head, most understanding and sympathetic of nymphs, is like a pudding. Hundreds of things to do with things military are awaiting my attention and I can't think where to begin. As a matter of fact I am one of the most hopeless soldiers I've ever met. Tomorrow I am going on 48 hours leave. I shall spend it at home and just relax. Shall I see thee there, beloved one? Are you honestly not fickle? Nonsense – all your sex is fickle; almost as fickle as mine. Blast this war. I have a glass of indifferent sherry beside me. I give you this toast. The sweetest lady in the land. Hm. I feel about 1% better.

I should like to see you very much. Quite honestly I believe we shall like each other very much, though we should be careful to meet under suitable circumstances. That is awfully important. Certainly you must sing for me one day I do not like thee Dr Fell,
The reason why I cannot tell,
But this I know and know full well,
I do not like thee Dr Fell.
Silly isn't it? Some day we will swap exquisite poems but at the moment I'm afraid my soul is quite dead.

My dearest Vari, I am so very tired of this wasteful war. It is a most aggravating thing and has already gone on for too long. Remind me to stop it will you? What actually are you going to do in the future, school having been left, as they say in Rome.

I must end and go and have some dinner and bid you a tender farewell wishing you, mademoiselle, de la bonne chance. Do not forget, if you are going to write to me again after December 5th to send it home –

With b.c. d'amour

Jean

391/98ᵗʰ 7d RegtRA,
Shillingstone,
Dorset

15 December 1941

Dere Vary,

For the last three years life has been hardly worth living. You have diligently neglected me. I am almost moved to write a bitter tirade to the effect that men he whairi of Mhairi because she is so vhairi contrhairi. Someone has got a radiogram and lots of records. At the moment it is playing Dvorak's New World Symphony. Parts of it make me literally wriggle with pleasure. Absolutely superb. Perhaps you know it.

<u>Tuesday night</u>. I got your letter this morning and so absolve you from the charge of neglect. I am most awfully sorry to hear about Hamish.[7] Poor Vari. I do hope you hear good news. I very much regret never having met him. I was at home on the last weekend in November but never went to the Kils' I'm afraid. I expected to meet Mr Kil at the Greyhound (which you probably know!) on the Monday but it was raining so hard and was so

---

[7] My brother in the Air Force, who was shot down but fortunately ended up a prisoner of war.

foggy that he never appeared. What a ludicrous war this is. The waste sometimes makes me very frightened.

The waste of time and youth and beauty and innocence. And then again I think that it's me that's wasting the time and that life is what you make it. But this is not true. Dreamy undergraduate or so-called efficient solder? Cambridge digs or a tin hut? Scotland, the Lakes, North Wales, Cornwall Devon and Surrey or Sussex
or Larkhill? Going slowly, luxuriously through French villages in the summer on a bike or rushing through an armoured carrier? Austria in the Spring, the Italian Lakes, the German beer gardens – there was so much to do and so little time to do it and over 2 years have slipped away.

War is so sordid and cheap until you are fighting for your life and for your freedom. They day that we are invaded and the enemy has landed and is pushing on to London from the South and from the East, and the English have given way before the initial shock because they are only half awake – on that day there will be or could be something more worth doing than all the rest – that will make the thought of lazy holidays ridiculous and all previous experiences a childishness of long ago. There is, or course – it's such a platitude – great nobility in the small standing up to the great: David against Goliath, the Greeks against the Persians, one man against many. It's a noble thing to be the underdog and stand to fight but a most dangerous. It was typical of Britain to disarm herself when she did – an ideal that is most unpractical, and experience seems to show that superiority of machinery is the decisive factor of modern war. This is a depressing conclusion for those with noble poetic and heroic souls! But the fight of one against many is still noble even if the one loses. *"For how can man die better than facing fearful odds?"* there is a wonderful verse in a poem of Houseman's called *The Oracles*. It describes how, on the news that the Persians were descending on Greece, the Greeks sent to inquire of the oracle what should be done. The oracle is not too optimistic.

"the King with half the East at heel is marching from lands of morning,
His armies drink the rivers up, their shafts benight the air and he that stands will die for nought, and back,
There's no returning
The Spartans on the sea west rock sat down and combed their hair."

These encouraging thoughts you must forgive. I think you will know what I mean and how I feel. I resent being made to grow up before I should! They are probably induced by Beethoven's Emperor Concerto, which has now finished so I will endeavor to be a little less gloomy.

I am happy as such a malcontent can be down here in Dorset. It is a wee village and the country is beautiful. After Larkhill it is as perfect a change as one could wish. Unfortunately the inhabitants though charming are either 6 or 60.

There are no young men and maidens here. And as we are completely cut off from everywhere one is apt to wish for some nice pleasant company. I shan't be home for Christmas but hope to be for the New Year. What do you want for Christmas? This is an absurd question, as you obviously have no sensible ideas on the subject. I shall probably write pages and pages of this as I am orderly officer and shall perforce stay till 12 o'clock to turn out the guard. This is a very aggravating thing as I shall be in a stupid semi-soporific state. At the moment dinner calls me, so farewell for a few minutes while I feed my face.

Well I have now had dinner. The gramophone is playing *Danse Macabre*. Wrong. He news is now being uttered by Wilfred Pickles. After the news I shall put on the *Eroica*. Aren't I lucky? You know this war is really rather funny. When even Hawaii is involved I had quite decided to go there after the war and recuperate. It seems I shall have to make it Tahiti after all.

Our Battery Commander, a charming bloke, had a bad motorcycle accident the other day and fractured his skull and is on the danger list. The Battery is suffering accordingly as I am at the moment cting Troop Commander!

It now appears to be Thursday. How I can have prevented my eager heart from expressing itself to you, I just cannot imagine. Christmas really is close. I had no idea it was only a week. My dear Vari, may god be thanked ye're a bonnie Scots lassie, for I'll be sending you a present at the New Year instead of Chrismas. But right at the moment I can't thin just what I'll be sending you. Girls are very very difficult. The battery is doing a concert on Christmas day. As it will be done by with from and for the battery, it will probably be a very rude show. The officers are meant to be doing a sketch but the fun will start when everybody gets a warmth of Dorset ale inside of them and calls upon us unfortunate stooges to entertain them – not my strong point so good deal of beer will probably be drunk by both sides. We are trying to get some champagne for our dinner and a 20 lb turkey. The champagne will remind me of you. Dear Bubbly. My pen having run out or penno excurrito as the red Indians say. I'm perforce take up my pencil.

I can't help feeling this is rather a chequered epistle. You will be home by the time you get this. Judging by the state of the post in this rural district you'll probably have gone back again. I was always told it was a woman's privilege to change her mind but it's going a bit far when one says in a letter I am not sending a photograph. I am sending you a photograph. I am not sending you a photograph. I'm willing to admit you to the twenties but one shouldn't go senile until after 60. They're playing Tchaikvsky's No.1 piano concerto. My god, it's good. I always feel he's rather sensual and more personal than Beethoven. A friend of mine up at Cambridge always used to say if you put a girl and a boy in a room and played Tchaikovsky to them, they'd be in each other's arms before the afternoon was over. That was Cambridge!

Thou dost bid me explain what I mean by meeting under suitable circumstances. Well I have a craven and utterly loathsome sort of belief founded on experience through the ages, that when you are looking forward to a thing very much it always turns out to be a flop and vice versa. So I can always tell whether or not a thing is going to be a flop by searching to see if I am inwardly looking forward to it. Meeting you couldn't be a flop because you're far too nice and you talk too much, but I want our meeting to be a riot. An absolute riot in London with one hell of a party. This is to take place about Christmas 1942. This is FATE and not to be interfered with. So send me a photograph to while away the intervening year! A year sounds an impossible time so I think I shall have to adjust fate to suit the times. Oh dear what a life.

It has suddenly got very cold here. I think it must be pleasant in the East. Though I have no wish to fight the Japanese who would almost certainly do something <u>horrible</u> to you if they captured you. This belief s so founded on the unchallenged verity of the history of Dr Fu.

Bunsi Kibichi Little girl – which I'm told means good luck. Good night or nicht or nach or nuit or nox or Greek.

    Je t'embrasse

        Jean

The C.O.'s Office
Westdown, WILTS.
31/12/41

My little cabbage, what a very nice present. How very sweet of you. We are back at Larkhill for a week's firing practice and I am Regimental orderly Officer and it is pretty cold. Your present is wrapped around my heart and is probably saving me from death by freezing. Therefore you have saved my worthless life therefore miserable servant thank honourable miss from bottom of vile heart. I am sending you, late, not a rosy wreath but a rather dull slip of paper. Unless you are minded to get something else, will you get an HMV record No: D.B.3077 which is a curious tune called Danse Macabre by Saint Saens. I think it is rather fun and would like you to get it out of a morbid sense of subtle irony. If you can imagine what that means you are even cleverer than my conception of you which would be impossible anyway. This firing camp I am afraid is turning me mad. I believe I told you I was liable to these awful fits of lunacy from time to time. Well I suppose this is one of those times. I do hope that you have – sorry, had – a good time over New Year and Christmas. I am really terrible sorry about this present of mine being so criminally late. Forgive me. There is now such a terrible noise going on that I can't concentrate what few faculties I have left on anything at all. For a time nothing happens at all and then suddenly 6 telephones ring and you pick up one at random and find you're keeping five brigadiers waiting on all the others. It is rather like a silly film and very soon I shall start lifting up the receiver and saying "No", and putting the receiver down again. I did like your Christmas card enormously. It decorates my bedside table in Lord Chesterfield's mansion. You know I can't believe I have told you about Lord Chesterfield. There are a lot of things I could tell you about, if only I were not losing my reason. This firing camp is really hell and relentless life on a volcano which is eternally liable to erupt. The volcano being the powers that be. Also we work all over the weekend which is against my principles entirely. I shall welcome the return to Shillingstone. This is now some time later and I am standing up waiting for the Battery Commander to come and dish out curses all round. We have now been waiting for ½ hour and my foot is going rapidly to sleep. Also I get hungry. The slight red blot on the right is not actually by heart's blood but a fragment of ink, red. This page appears to be a little grubby. We had a magnificent time over Christmas. We ate turkey and drank champagne. I drank your health you will be glad to hear and doubtless your health has improved accordingly. In the evening we made a lot of noise and had a most dangerous game of rugger in a room with a lot of jagged bits jutting out. The concert was a great success due to the profusion of beer I rather suspect. Another bloke and I did an incredibly witty Western Bros. sketch or dialogue composed by that brilliant young composer, me. I think I must go to Claridges sometime. What I remember of it is very pleasant, and it's the weak-minded memories. Very sweet. London on New Year's Eve would have delighted you. We went to see Quiet Week-End. It was one of the best plays I have seen –absolutely grand. Leaving Wyndhams at about 8 o'clock we took a taxi to the Lansdown

Restaurant. This unfortunately was all booked up and had been refusing people for 10 days. The bloke said very excitedly we'd get nothing to eat anywhere in London. We said in our best American: "Aw to Hell with that" and got another taxi. We said "The 3 Vikings". The man had never heard of it but I directed him roughly. On the way we ran into the Piccadilly area. Huge traffic jams and the streets packed with people singing and shouting and trying to get into and onto our taxi. Lots of light and a fine moonlit night. It was like the Armistice Day will be, and met with my full approval. We found the 3 Vikings eventually and to my relief got a table. I had almost abandoned hope seeing all those thousands of people outside. It was a grand evening. I hope you too had a merry time, dear puella.

Talking of the Rhapsody in Blue I got it for Joan's Christmas present. I am very fond of it. It's the HMV one with Gershwin at the piano and I think the best. But as for what I should get with £1 token, well that ain't so easy. One simply doesn't know where to begin. Hungarian Rhapsody No:2. Ballet Egyptian. Tchaikovsky's Italian Caprice. Oh there are hundreds. Practically all Gershwin The Man I Love (grand tune preferably sung by some peculiar person such as Maxine Sullivan) and tunes like Night and Day. The thing to do is to go into a gramophone shop and spend a whole day just listening to records. Take a picnic lunch.

Believe me I need little pressing to come to Scotland. I think it's the most terrific place that ever was. So please return the good wishes sent to me by your people. Here's wishing the Falconer family a happy New Year.

It occurs to me that this letter is 90% illegible. I am sitting in a very queer position as usual and am very much asleep.

I shall be back at Shillingstone next Thursday if you intend ever to write to me again. I am afraid this is a very dull letter. It's quite fatal trying to do anything in an Officers' Mess. The atmosphere is cuttable with a knife and one gets drowsier and drowsier. So outside it's too cold and inside it's too hot. Silly isn't it? It will be nice when spring comes again, and then Summer. I saw Mrs Kil who said Sheila was looking very fit. What a tremendous bit of luck getting posted to Hook.

With reference to this Danse Macabre I think you will find the first record the most exciting and the second side rather disappointing, Have you got a radiogram that plays 8 at a time? That's definitely the thing to have.

Well my young poetess, I will bid you a very fond farewell, thank you again for your present and wish you even more good wishes.

Maximo amore

Johannis

391/98th Field Regt
Shillingstone, DORSET

January: 18th 1942

Dear Lady,

You are superb. Being quite the little gentleman, I withstood the mad overwhelming impulse to rent the arrogant envelope that dared withhold from my sight your peerless beauty.

> There was a young lady called Mhair,
> Who was photographed by her Paphair,
> The published result
> Makes the male heart exult,
> So she's now sought by men near and fhair.
> Hhair! Hhair!

My apologies for this extravaganza – due to Sabbath post-prandial indigestion. but my god what a little dumpling – I feel that with such muscled legs and such determined cheeks you should have gone far, by 1942, as an amazon cross-country runner. Anyhow the surprise as we say in military parlance, was complete. You are a very naughty little girl. You may once more (it speaks most ill of you the number of times I have to say this) consider yourself spanked.

Nothing at all exciting has happened since I last wrote to you. I am in a particularly weak state owing to an overwhelming tragedy with which I was on Friday smitten down. As I result I can only hobble about and my legs will probably be slightly stiff for the rest of my life. It was due entirely to evil circumstances. There was Regimental Cross Country Run to select the 15 best runners to enter for a Corps Run. Well each battery had to send 9 men and 1 officer. As everybody is on leave this ghastly fate fell to my lot. There are a lot of things I do badly and there are a lot of things I loathe doing. Cross Country Running I loathe above all things and do very badly. It was over 6m miles – just to keep up interest the course went through a river about a thousand years wide and twenty feel deep, under every barbed wire fence in Dorset, through hitherto unpenetrated jungle, through an occasional snow drift and over one or two small icebergs. I may say we had had marmalade pudding for lunch. It only took about 24 hours in all. If thou wouldst pray, pray for my soul. My body is past praying for. I ended up 21 out of 33 which was damn good. The 12 I beat had only got one leg. Since then my one desire has been to sleep. Even this was denied me due to the following adverse factors.

a) "Strange Conflict" a very strange book by Dennis Wheatley which terrified me and which was so exciting I went on reading it till 2 a.m.
b) There was nothing left in the Mess to eat last night so we went out to Blandford and had an extremely good dinner which turned itself into a party which went on rather late.

c) I had to get up at 7 this morning and can't go to bed till after midnight as I am accursed orderly officer. Grrr. Next Saturday we are having a Regimental Offices Dance. There are awful affairs. The Colonel invites all officers. This involves paying some enormous sum and getting courtmartialled if you don't turn up. Very fortunately a girl (desperately attractive, fatally fascinating) I used to know very well in my youth (ages ago) is in Blandford for the week so I shall I hope have an anchor in the regimental storm. Dancing under most circumstances i.e. when I'm sober) simply appalls me. This, I trust, discourages your belie that I am a romantic young man. My appreciation of The Man I love is purely aesthetic. Really, darling, you get the strangest notions. But then you are of course a very strange person. An equally idiotic person and myself made Lady Patricia an apple pie bed when in jolly mood one night. This had terrific reverberations and for a week nobody could go to bed without making sure there were no pins etc. in the bed. Our unfortunate Battery Commander as also victimized by nobody knows quite who by. So Lord Chesterfield's mansion has seen some unearthly and bourgeois behavior of late. Lord C. is the bloke on whom we be billeted.

I may say I am madly jealous of sub lieutenant Michael and shall certainly arrange a duel at the first opportunity. My face, could you see it, is a shade of green. I must now hasten to correct one or two inexactitudes in your account of the famous wedding. You looked so shy when you pushed Jimmie forward to say "Bride or Groom?" To be precise I was rather drunk. I had spent the morning endeavouring to bolster up old Tigs' courage. This involved the consumption of a certain amount of liquor. (There was an air raid alarm in the middle I seem to remember so we thought perhaps nobody would be able to get to London anyhow!) and then we went and had a party at the Savoy where we consumed a little more. My capacity s not at that time fo the proportions it has now attained.

I don't believe you were ever too shy to do anything. Don't be, Vari. There are probably more – but no hap, I pass them over.

I do wish I could come and see if the braes and banks really do blume sal fair but the roi de la royaume just won't let me get time to do anything worth doing. How about coming down South. I will meet you in May or August 1942. That's an order. I suppose you are now back at ecole, no doubt ordering around unfortunate little girls. If only I were not so aggravatingly idle I would write an autobiography. It is most tiresome. It would be a very successful book and I should have as frontispiece a picture of me when young face down on a rug. I would sell you a copy. I am in the process of writing a long and somewhat immature poem. At the moment it is scattered about in bits on the back of various envelopes and mere bills and other waste paper. I am due for 7 days at the commencement of February. That'll be pleasant. I hope there may perhaps be some skating. That would be even more pleasant. I am appalled at the thought of of all the letters I have to write. The mood is not on me.

How are you Mhairi? How tall are you, how much do you weigh, what size shoes do you take, do you eat soup out of an old eggtimer, do you walk along backwards looking between your legs, do you eat bacon with sugar tongs? If YES – Then you will have 37 children and marry a one-legged sailor who plays the violin. If NO your head will drop off on Wednesdays. i am completely devoid of ideas, so will bid you goodnight, my sweet, and dreams of home.

With lots of love,

Yours faithfully

<u>Me</u>

391/98th7d Regt RA
Shillingstone
Dorset

10 February 1942

My very dear Mhairi,

I am so very sorry for not having written for so very long. I'm not sure quite how long it is as I have mislaid your letter. Actually it reposes on my dressing table up at the house and is accordingly out of range at the moment. I returned from 7 days last night to find myself orderly officer for today. This heartless custom always greets one on returning from leave. So instead of getting up just before eleven o'clock you get up just before seven and instead of going to bed drunk at 5 in the morning you go to bed sober at half past midnight.

C'est la vie (as one might say). I thoroughly enjoyed my leave you will be glad to hear. I spent un certain amount de temps at the capital, saw Blithe Spirit which is very funny, and danced at the Piccadilly. There are 3 interesting dance tunes: Elmer's Tune, which I think is good; something to do with Dust or Sand and Shoes; and Concerto for Two which is nothing either more or less than the opening tune of Tchaikovsky's No. 1 Piano Concerto. Pretty cool of somebody. This is going to be a most dull letter as I do not feel a flow of inspiration. I have just bought a motorcycle for £15. At the moment my bank balance is £7 and I've the whole of this month to go so it may be rather awkward. It's a grand bike. It was born in 1922 so it's older than you, my sweet, and almost as old as my senile self. I managed to start it and rode it up and down the road but it emitted such enormous clouds of blue smoke that I feared it would blow up any moment or at lest put an acrid smoke screen about Shillingstone, so I took it and began taking it to pieces. Unfortunately darkness overtook me and I was left in rather an awkward position with screws and things all over the place. From all these operations we sustained only minor injuries – to wit: one wrist burnt on an exhaust pipe and one inch of dirt over the whole person and battledress of 4th Lieut. John Cuthbert. What is your other name, I can't remember but believe you once told me.

While on leave I skated twice. On Sunday it was absolutely grand. We had a large pond for the exclusive use of 3 of us. The ice was zery goot. Did you invite me to Scotland once? And did you offer me 2 lorryloads of fruit? Alas you'll not even be able to supply soap now. Que la view est formidable! If my chuck you ever write to me gain, will you write to me at The Haven, West Parade, Rhyl, North Wales. I am, going there for a 3 weeks course on Saturday next. It will doubtless be very old and very wet and very muddy. Encore je dis c'est la vie. Almost as happy a knack of rhyming as you have. I seem vaguely to remember love on a beach or something which you perpetrated in your last missive. The memory is most stimulating. I must refer to the passage when I go to bed. When. For it's only 10 o'clock. I shall put on Beethoven's 7th. Someone is drawing a sketch of me from the far corner of the room. He has forbidden me to move my legs and consequently I an suffering untold agonies of cramp.

Our battery is once again having a complete reshuffle of offices and all sorts of queer things are happening. One cannot go away for a few days without returning to find everything in chaos. Heigho. The 7th is now in full swing. It is a lovely symphony. I wonder how long it will before it is jazzed. Some bright American has already done the fifth! I saw Mr Kil and Mrs Kil when at old Thames Ditton. They were both flourishing but are losing Eva their cook whom you may or may not remember. She is going I think into the Wrens. Old Bill Prior is still intact. He says he really can't tell how many peaches he'll be able to produce this year. It occurred to me that probably the production would lie greater if you weren't there to entice, Evelike, your unsuspecting boyfriends into the rose garden and eat them all. (Them = peaches, not boyfriends)

Alas I shall not see you in April unless the gods are peculiarly propitious. Scotland is altogether too far away and I shall be leaveless like Adam and eve before the Fall of Man. Ha1Ha! Clever that.

I am getting a little soporific. Be an angel and write me a nice long letter at Rhyl. You might even enclose your first pair of socks or tell me what size shoes you took at the age of 3 and 3 months.

Oh Vari Vari what a waste this war is. The seventh symphony is in its third movement. In an hour I shall turn out the guard.

Goodnight, little Ladye

Affectueusement, ton John

The Haven
West Parade
Rhyl
March 1st 1942

Well, Fayre Ladye,

Once more I seem to have been rather a long time in replying to yours of the 17th ult. I just hate to think of the roses fading from your cheeks. Of course I was forgetting – the Fascinating Blonde. As a matter of fact I never went to the dance with her – so life has really lost its meaning for me. I was of course a little cheered by the Exquisite Auburn Haired fire at the Piccadilly, but for ever I shall carry the scars of disappointment in my soul. I am sitting on a very cramped armchair which prevents my writing being even faintly legible. I am well at fighting a great battle against the arrival of a hostile cold. My gallant defense consists of drinking an enormous amount of whiskey on the slightest provocation and staying in bed this morning till lunch time. But if one rides about in a Bren Carrier all day long in the rain, snow, sleet, ice, blizzard, tempest old uncle tom cobleigh and all what can one expect I ask you. My motorbike when I left it was in pieces but I left instructions with one of our mechanics to put it together again and apparently he has taken his pals along so half the mechanical brains of the Sussex Yeomanry is engaged upon the task. It ought to go rather well at the end. At my last meeting it sent out a very thick and very smelly smoke screen from both exhausts. It shall be called Percy but it shall not have a bottle of beer broken over it. Its owner will deputise and break the bottle inside himself. Before I forget, I shall be leaving here next Saturday March 5th and I am not going back to Shillingstone. I don't know what my new address will be so perhaps dearest you'll write home. But how too sweet of you. What is this curious word that looks like SCUNNER? Is it SCUNNER? What an outlandish word. It is Maori? And as for not wanting boyfriends – well I just give up. Psychology is in despair. Safe in the Magic of my Woods as far as I remember is rather a poor poem. I suppose the sentiment is genuine enough but the verse is horrible, and Vari, most inapplicable. if you haven't written to Tigs (I expect you have by now!) do wish him all the best from me. I wonder how he's enjoying life.

Someone on the wireless is talking drivel. This is not unusual in these days, I find. There are a lot of officers sitting round the fire in various stages of somnolence and somebody is snoring vulgarly. I feel somnolent myself after my hard morning's sleep, and quite uninspired. We work pretty hard here on the whole but we waste an awful lot of time, and I don't think the course is very well run. Anyhow a lot of it is the same as the stuff we did when I was here before and I don't hesitate to say that it's just a wee bit boring, wee lassie. I had rather roam the hills, look down on the lochs and lie in the heather in this fair company. I really do want to spend several months in Scotland in June and July and August and September. So after the war I'll come up and you can find me a job as a shepherd which I should do very well. Alternatively your father can pay me a very high salary for looking after his daughter and keeping her out of mischief. I should certainly very soon bore you to death which would perhaps be unfair to the world in general and a great pity.

This is so dull I blush with shame. Maybe next time I write inspiration will have returned –

>Farewell, my dear, and look both ways when you cross the road.

>With love John

OFFICERS' MESS,
BRAMLEY,
BASINGSTOKE, HANTS.

PHONE: BRAMLEY GREEN 250.   Sat: 11th April 1942

My charming young lady,

You must excuse this unworthy crest – I am here for a week learning about ammunition. That's the idea anyway. In fact, my putrid brain is entirely incapable of taking in any of the sanguinarified chemical formulae concerned therewith. It's in short, a horrrrible week I'm spending. Luckily we feed very well, having (an oddity this) a most capable staff of ATS. So I grow fat and uninteresting. I hope to pinch a couple of days leave at the end of the week. So I shall endeavor not quite to lose my soul. The Mess in which I am sitting is of the traditional type. If one does the Times crossword (which I do) an AT appears and croaks: "Has any gentleman got the Times please?" I always reckon that title excludes me but it's an odd habit of the army to call the most unlikely people gentlemen on every possible occasion. Well I say nothing and the AT adds by way of explanation: "The Colonel wants it." So I haven't in this feudal world, a chance of survival, and hand it over. Anyone who comes stamping in when the News is on is met by a powerful barrage of hostile eyes. Sort of H.M. Bateman drawing. Tonight I breezed in and accidentally hit the fire gong which reverberated dismally in the silence. I grinned amiably and made to attempt to stop it and ws met with astonished glances of horror from the old fossils.

The Isle of Wight is going to be lovely when summer comes. We had a few gorgeous days in March – did I tell you? – and I climbed round the cliffs and sunbathed in a little cove. It was boiling hot. The weather since has been pretty foul. Very gusty and rather cold. We've been working night and day literally, so this is by way of being a rest cure. I think I'd rather work! I had thought Bramley was about 4 miles from Guildford. So it is but that' another one. It would be.

Thank you Vari dear for your nice letter and the mysterious promise of food. You are very sweet and I do love eating.

Will you be all home on May 10th or thereabouts. I intend having 10 days leave. To do this you have to be more than 90 miles away from where you're stationed. Therefore with your permission, I will give your address. If you'll be home then I'll come and see you for a day or two if you could tolerate it – if not I shall just have to practice a deceit. Fortunately I've got no conscience anyway.

The summer is going to be grand. The English winter certainly makes you appreciate the other end of the year. Summer = warmth, freedom, blue sky, gold sun, green grass, pink strawberry ices, brown faces, white roads, white rocks, white seagulls, black nights and a lovely healthy, happy, hungry clean feeling inside you. Walks before breakfast, the sun on the breakfast table, after a decent interval, shoppin in the town, the bathe, the enormous picnic lunch, the rather solemn and whimsical and utterly satisfactory post-picnic conversation. The lazy lying on the beach, the walk through cool woods, tea at a farmhouse under the hill, staying to chat with the farmer and his children and grandchildren and his wife, and the walking back for supper. After supper walking along the cliff just as the sun goes down – strolling on till the sun has really gone down and the Evening Star has come out, until night itself appears. This is really romantic. Let's draw a decent veil. Such is summer. Don't be alarmed by details such as – having to parade after breakfast, having to parade after lunch, having to parade after tea, and (being orderly officer in any case) being unable to leave the billet area. Man's spirit, as comfortable old philosophers assure us, has no difficulty

whatsoever in surmounting barbed wire fences and man made institutions such as Regimental orders. It may interest you to know I have first had this sarcasm weighted. It was 20 tons. No, Vari, life is very well worth living in the summer. But the spring can be cruel, can't it? "April is the cruellest month." Spring is hell if you can't have what you want – and who can? And spring is hell if you're lonely – and who isn't?

You know I have a feeling I ought to be reading all about gunpowder and ammonium sulphates. But it's only a very minor feeling and I'm not interested n it. There's a dirty little cinema here but it played the Warsaw Concerto, bless it. It's a grand, catching, attractive tune. We had a performance of Waterloo Bridge. The most sentimental film ever made, wonderfully well acted I think – you feel a nervous wreck and a miserable broken man when you come out. But all the solders roared and screamed and shouted at the most sentimental and harrowing moments so some of the gripping pathos and heart-string-rending-tear-making scenes were somewhat ruined. And whenever Mr Taylor kissed Miss Leigh (which was not infrequently) he did so to the applause of the whole garrison.

I hope you had a riotous time on April 2nd, and did not overdo the champagne, you old toper. Young ladies of 21 in my day never drank at all. Flashback – that sentence reminds me of Cambridge. Heigh – times do move.

I have come to a violent cessation of inspiration probably brought about by some very indifferent beer which stands at my elbow. The dear boy has such a delicate stomach.

I feel cheerful tonight (for a change – le malheureux?) and I hope my dear that you do too.

With lots of love (that should do it)

Jean

10/5/42

391/98th Fd Regt RA
Merley House
Wimborne
Dorset

Vari dear, find it in your large heart to forget I haven't written for so many moons. We've been enormously busy, having had half the Battery away on embarkation leave. I'm going next Saturday for 14 days. As is the usual custom of the British army, the powers that be chose the time when half or even 2/3 of the caps were away, to have demonstrations, firing practices, schemes, exercises and all the other delights with which the soldier is entertained. It was really rather fun – we found ourselves driving guns and tractors and doing a lot of very odd things.

Well Vari, it looks as though, like everybody else, we're going abroad at last. I must confess I'm glad, though I have no doubt whatsoever that I shall be as homesick as hell when I get there. And this Island (I'm writing this just before leaving for Wimborne) is the most lovely place on earth. It is just spring here – awfully late in arriving but very beautiful. The views are the most peaceful and exciting imaginable. We have been living a peaceful happy life untroubled by outside influences (almost anyway!) and eating and drinking like kings. We've been bathing and sunbathing and dancing and having lots of fun. And we'll probably be eating sand and drinking coconut milk in the future, but I'm still not really sorry. In fact as I said before, I'm glad. On the other hand of course we may be hanging around in this country for years. Well as long as they give us 7 days leave every other week, I shan't grumble. I can't help feeling that Winter is the time to go abroad. I rather think the summer should be spent here.

I must terminate this brief epistle as we are moving from YE DELECTIBLE ISLAND in not many minutes. Et mon coeur s'est casse.

Take good care of yerself chum – I'll write again when I'm on leave and endeavor to be un peu plus interessant.

Je t'embrasse, mon amour,

John

Woodside
Weston Park
Thomas Ditton

May 19, 1942

Sweetheart, here's your letter. You have just written me the nicest letter I have ever had, and, I think, the most honest. You deserve the same from me but you probably won't get it. Since I have known you I have fallen in love just four times. This, I am told, is quite the thing to do when one is 21. Before I met you I had fallen in love just twice. But never, Vari, never has anyone been able to write letters like you. Thank god, my dear, you have a heart of gold, with your head way up amid the dangerous exciting stars and your feet firmly rooted in good Scottish earth as ever any women had. You may be under 17 but you've the insight of the devil – you know half the time exactly what I am thinking and I know you know, so sometimes I write the most inconsequential and illogical things just to get you muddled up. We are so very much alike, both so very sensitive. When I was at school I used to curse at being so sensitive but since I have gained years of discretion (damn nearly a year my love) I have somewhat recanted. There is such beauty in the world, and so few who see it.

When I write to you about our island, the old island of the monks, I am suffering from what Freud would call something obscene, and what other psychologists would call nostalgia but which you and I know is a heartbreaking desire for what might have been, a sort of Peter Pan agony at the relentless passage of time and the cruelty of a cynical fate that sends a war to waken us to the urgency of life and to say – when we have awoken t it – 'oh no, you're too late now, off to the army with you where we'll kill your soul with boredom or hour body with bullets. And Vari? Why she shall have time to think on how nice it would have been to go to the aux Moines. I hate this war because the only reason I sometimes think I like the army is because it has destroyed in me my sensitiveness. I can go out drinking and dancing (after a fashion) and think I am having a hell of a time. And all the while the figs on the aux Moines are growing ripe and splashing onto the dusty roads where dogs lazily taste them with their tongues. And in Scotland the sun is shining on heather and lochs where (I have no doubt) famous highland regiments practice combined operations on a miniature scale. Vari, we are so slow to learn and then we are so futile in the way we cry because we are too late.

They're playing Mozart's *Jupiter* Symphony on the wireless. My mood changes as often as the clouds pass across the sun. I don't begin to understand myself, I never know what I am going to do next. I should make a terrible husband for a girl. But if I come back from abroad and haven't married a nurse out of gratitude, I will marry you like a shot, Vari darling – if you'll have me. And this at the risk of being sued for breach of promise. I'm £13 overdrawn anyway, so it's not worth considering!

The country's beautiful – everything is so peaceful and everyone so charming. I wish to god it was the continent we were invading and not the desert or whatever else one invades in this horribly vague war. I shall think of you, when I think of love, as a girl who was very gar and very gentle., whose laughter was as bright and as impotent as Tinkerbell's and who couldn't pronounce simple words like horrible.

I grow tired of saying this, but I'm the most undependable person on earth. For days or was it weeks, I didn't write to you to thank you for your parcel and your letters which were sweet. I was busy, yes, but I could have written. Probably I was out enjoying myself – who knows? – and yet you say you understand, and I believe you.

If I should meet you this week I should say, "Vari, you are very understanding, by far the most understanding girl I know, and by far the nicest". If I should meet you when the war is over, I should try to be more eloquent. Even if it entailed muttering through my beard. Incidentally not the least of your charms is an ability to read my writing.

Won't you send me a photograph of yourself? Sweetheart, you must for the sake of your Greta Garbo coiffure, your rolling rs, your lovely country, your poetry, your grace your wit your charm your gaiety, your idiocy – my very much beloved lunatic.

Of course I may be here for years.

I should adore you to see me off but as we don't know when or where we're going from till we've gone it presents a rather knotty problem.

Take good care of yourself, darling, for you too are precious.

Je te definitely embrasse.

John

391/98 rd Rgt
Merley House
Wimborne
Dorsetshire
June 1st '42

Dear Miss Faulkner

I hope you are well. I am writing to tell you my address as I don't think you know it me not having wrote to you before from here.

Oh darling it would be grand to see you. You are the most adorable girl and you write the most delicious letters. And I've got a Warsaw concerto and it is so marvelous that I used to play it round and round and oval (ha! Ha! That fooled you) and just couldn't get sick of it.

When feeling bad, I used to put on the Warsaw concerto and follow it with the slow movement of Beethoven's fifth. The effect was almost instantaneous. You are even sweeter than I thought you were (as Jack Hulbert once quoth) for suggesting that your longsuffering father should bring me a record. Photographs are awful aren't they? But I do so want to see even approximately what you look like that I am sure you won't refuse me. And remember my love that while I may not go for three months, I may go tomorrow, so let not too much time pass through the glass he said mixing with unnerving fingers his fascinating metaphors. I have had a photograph of myself taken in a sports jacket. This was done under extreme pressure. My father, like Mr Darling, said 'all right Johnnie Wonnie, so have your photo taken and Daddy'll have his taken'. We did and if the photograph portrays the mood we were in it ought to be rather a classic. This is however quite by the way.

I am going to make a suggestion that will clear all doubts from our minds about me being a sentimentalist. Send me, and I will send you, a silver or substitute plaque or disc upon which shall be inscribed on one side, the name and number etc. for purposes of identification in case we get blown up, and on the other some simple but heart rendering message such as "fair hair is green, my dear" or "Jon likes Vari ever so" this will be worn round the neck until such time as hostilities (oh blast Hitler) have ceased and we are introducing each other to each other after all these years. I think this is a wonderful idea for a sentimentalist. Do you? I will endeavor to find a chain as well if possible. Wimborne is not very prolific in jewellers' shops and they never seem to open anyway, but will doubtless find a way. One side will have to be left unengraved of course as though there is so little we don't know about each other (yeah?) I don't know your registration number and you don't know mine. Actually it is 193460 and my religion is (actually sun worshipper) C.E. If you tell me your registration number quickly I'll have it put on. Do you see what I'm aiming at or am I quite alone in my rather woolly reasoning, no?

My sweet, there are so many things we have to do. To walk all day over your hills, above your lochs, knee deep, or ankle deep in heather and bog. To walk in sunshine and in spring rain and t get so hungry we can hardly wait till midday till we eat our lunch. To walk along the beach and to climb around the point through the splashing sea to a bay where the cliffs are tall and white and concave and seagulls live (Bembridge has the most glorious bays – I think I must have told you); to lie in the sun and pull each other's hair and make up limericks. To walk on the downs and drink cider in a Devonshire farmhouse and beer in a Sussex village. To watch cricket matches, to go to church on Sunday some place where the vicar is an old unspoilt simple man who won't try and draw a moral from why we won or lost the battle but who will give us the peace of god and send us into the country which is the best thing he made. To picnic in pine trees and drive to a roadhouse were the car park is full of cars and there is dancing inside and laughter and lots of silly thoughtless, have-a-good-time people making whoopee; to drive home in the night, fast, in an open car through woods and over heather, along wide bypasses, over railway bridges and through towns. We have got so much to do in England. To go up to London in the afternoon and shop. To buy you dresses, to hear gramophone recordings at H.M.V., to watch the people that pass and wonder where they go - the slim legged fashionable Bond street ladies, the foreigners and Jews in the Strand Palace, the interesting people in the Strand – to see people rushing in the underground – but all this will be changed maybe.

We've got to have tea where a 3 piece orchestra plays Victorian tunes; three middle aged ladies dressed in long ugly brown dresses that match the colour of the piano the cello and the violin they play. We must go and have cocktails at the Café

Royal and dinner, oh certainly we must have dinner at Claridges. And what theatre would madame like to be taken to? Musical comedy? Shakespeare? Ballet? The latest thriller? Or the play that all the critics hail as the greatest since *Mourning Became Electra*?

Anyhow we chose right because we both enjoyed it, so let's go and dance. Most of the nightclubs have been bombed and the rest spoiled by the war so where shall we go? Let's ask the commissionaire – we swap his good wishes for half a crown and get into the taxi he hails for us. Vari dear, you're so tired at 4 in the morning that I almost carry you to the Corner House at Leicester Square where dissolute young London sits huddled around Bacon and Eggs and Coffee trying not to be sick. So we drive home and someone at home lets us in with the milk.

Next day we're rather tired so we sleep till lunchtime. And we drive to Dorking and have tea at the Olde Mill, feeling rather ill, deliciously vague and very happy. We watch the sun set over Martha's Chapel at Newlands Corner, have some lager at the hotel and drive home early to bed. The sun in the morning is so hot we go on the river and tied up to a willow we talk such rot the swans come to listen. Or is it the sandwiches in your lap? They come so close to you I get jealous and push them off with a paddle. Silly tactless swans that don't know when they're not wanted. In the golden evening I propel you up stream, beneath Hampton Court Bridge to the Mitre Hotel where we eat lobster and drink champagne. This is exciting and such fun; the waiters all look at us and smile and try to rival one another to help us. We stay there drinking Kummel till very late and even the swans are going to sleep and the only sound is a tired waiter clearing up the spoons and the fall of the weir at Hampton Lock. We punt down downstream at a snail's pace because the night is so beautiful and you are humming to the moon and we have both fallen in love with the stars. Old Charlie Elliot the boatman is sitting by his boathouse smoking his old pipe and he hears us coming from a long way off, and waves. He's in no hurry. We get home and cannot bear to say goodnight.

Sweetheart, there is much beauty, is there not, in all these things? Given, of course, a large powerful car, and lots of clothes and even more money, and heavenly weather. Oh dammit it's no less than we deserve.

This morning I went through a wood of pine trees and the smell of them took me seventy miles or so to the ile aux Mines and I remembered how you want me to take you there. Oh Vari of course I promise. It means peace, utter, uttermost peace. So peaceful that it makes me squirm to think of it. I shall take you there and you shall see.

Could you really tell when I had fallen in love – I don't know that you could – sometimes I just feel uninspired and dull and write awful letters. And anyway when I say fallen in love I don't mean it. In my young life I have fallen once in love. I used to think I should never know if I was really in love with a girl or if she was just trying to hook me for my money (young cynic!) but now of course I know. It is enough just to be near the person you love and you really want to do nothing except to please her (or presumably him!). It sounds so trite but it is so true. So falling in love with reference to the last 2 years = being attracted by.

Tom who is my bosom companion and shares a room with me is screaming at me to leave off writing to Dvorak (which is his pronunciation of Mhairi) and turn out the nameless light. I have agreed to finish this sheet and turn out the light. Always the little gent, Cooperation being my second name.

After the war I shall have no money at all and shall have no qualifications and no inclination to settle down to any job. I cannot see quite what will happen. And I am going round the world with a friend. We have sworn a very solemn oath. If I see you first I shall probably want to break it. Woman the temptress – oh Eve (Note: I wish I were Adam. End of note)

Little girl, I would like you to write regularly every hour, I would like to have a whole picture gallery of you, I would like, oh hell what wouldn't I like.

Good night darling. There is no translation for Je t'embrasse because the French are the greatest lovers on earth but we two on our old island would put the French to shame. We would because you're a very sweet enchantress and I sometimes think that I'm a poet inside of me.

Encore une fois, je t'embrasse, my lady desiree, don't overeat overdrink or oversing and beware of all hogoblins however innocent looking, please.

John

Merley House
Wimborne
14/6/42

Darling,

I think you're the nicest girl in all the world.

Here is the disc identity. It was astonishingly difficult to find one in London. I got it eventually in the Burlington Arcade, Oxford Street, and Bond Street having failed to oblige. He was a funny old man. I told him it was for a very attractive young lady and he must engrave it at once. This he agreed to do. I'm afraid his needle or style or whatever he operates with, went astray over one of the s's and the i of Maori.

He apologized profusely, said his hand was not as steady as it used to be and gave us his blessing. I send it with all my love.

This is perhaps the last letter I shall write you from England. You know darling I shan't be able to say when I am going, where I'm going from or where I'm going to. No tearful farewells, no waving crowds on the platform, no last embraces. You just go and nobody knows about it until you're gone. From henceforth my address will be
    391/98th field rgt RA
    C/O ARMY POST OFFICE 1755

I will write to you as often as I can and I know you will too. These intervening years (or tens of years!) will give us time to think of some really interesting things to do together – you and I. Meanwhile, dearest, you must have lots of fun. I know you will – you and Susan – there are so many ways of enjoying oneself – gay nights, midnight parties, London at dawn, things you can still do Vari, things you must do. Then you can write and tell me all (or almost all!) about them and I can think of you doing them and imagine I am doing them with you.

I am a Regimental Orderly office and I am sitting at the moment in the sun being eaten slowly to death by horseflies. Doubtless it is good practice. Having to stay in all day I may possibly write all the letters I ought to have written. I might have written the second epistle to the inhabitants of Ochtertyre and Sidon. But I don't think I will because I've little to say except that I really am falling in love with you by letter which is an awfully interesting phenomenon and such fun.

It's going to be grand seeing you again and dining at Claridges. We'll definitely make them play "The Nightingale Song in Berkeley Square", even if they have to shake off 10 years dust from the scores. And we'll definitely drink champagne and dance and sit around we to alone close kissed and eloquent of still replies at least one evening of the three months we have dedicated to each other. How say you pal? We have arranged to months, - a circular ticket via l'Ile aux Moines and bonnie Scotland. I think July in the Ile aux Moines, August in Scotland and September in and about London and Surrey. Then possibly June would have to be included for mucking about in Wales, the lakes, and England generally. I'm not sure of the morality of all this. Perhaps we could arrange a 3 months provisional marriage license – or should we have Sue and Tom as chaperones?

Au revoir, darling, and please look both ways when you cross the road, with all my love,

John

EMBARKATION
by Mhairi Falconer (aged 15)

It came –
That moment I had dreaded more than death,
Had caught up with my gleaming heart and mind,
And harsh reality had flung my dreams
Imagination's children, to the winds.
For though I knew the day would sometime dawn
When, by the winging sea and far bound ships
Our lives would once again be forced apart
(As fate had held them ere we bridged the gap)
Yet knew I not that these pained farewells
Would cross our lips before a kiss could seal
With pent up passion, all those silent vows
Which hearts in secret love can even share
But though there was not time for us to talk
Those secrets which we even more must hide
There can be no forgetting of the past
For it is printed deep within our hearts
You will remember this when shadows fall
And sultry heat gives place to silent night
For in the memories crowding through your brain
You will recall my whispered "j'attendrai"

39198th Field Rgt AA
C/o Army Post Office 1755
July 8th 1942

Volume II

Ma tres chere,

How are you? This is a great occasion. The idiot boy is about to be 22, what a terrible age it is. Also the vivacious lady, by the time she receives this will have ceased her scholastic pursuits and have launched out into the large and wicked world. Its wickedness is proverbial but its largeness I can vouch for. There's an awful lot of sea about the place. I suppose it is about a week or ten days since I wrote to you dates and times in general mean nothing to me – the way we juggle about with the clock is phenomenal. And I don't suppose you'll receive them in any sort of order. Qui sait, alors? C'est la guerre.

I don't think I ought to write on both sides of this paper – it's so thin, mais toujours l'economie. For my birthday tomorrow I shall have quite a party I think – alcohol is so deliciously cheap. I shall probably have to be reminded it's my birthday, I keep forgetting. Doubtless my drunken confederates will not let me forget the alcoholic aspect thereof. By the way, have you read *The Story of San Michelle*? If not, you really must, as you know without a shadow of doubt, it was written some ten or more years ago by Dr Axel Munthe. What now can I tell you about the sea that would hold you enthralled? Whether you like it or not this is how I spend my time:-

06.45 hours (that's army for ¼ to 7) a black boy knocks on the cabin door. Nobody hears and he goes on knocking quite unmoved for several minutes until someone says 'Come in'.

He will on no account enter before. I lay doggo once to see how long he'd keep it up. After 4 mins I am nearly driven mad and shouted out: "entre monsieur dans la chamber de madame". He entered quite unmoved. Next thing to do is to distribute a cup of tea to each inmate. If you are not awake once more he will just stand until you stir, he won't take any steps to wake you whatsoever You can't imagine how maddening this is. The tea has five dessertspoons of sugar in it and is quite undrinkable. If you say ' no sugar' he grins and promptly fills the basin with hot water. Very trying. Having eventually disposed of him we are invaded by batmen who crash around and knock everything over and drop polish all over the room. They disappear soon after 7 o'clock. We leap or rather roll wearily off our bunks at ¼ past and stagger up to the deck to do P.T. This is awful. You feel so limp with the heat and smell of cooking and old socks that rises from the bowels of the ship that you try and get to the very back of the class. To your dismay you find the colonel is also hiding back there and you have to make an effort. You rush madly down when it's all over in order to get a bath.

At the bottom of the stair way a boy has covered the floor with soap and water. You jump in the middle of this and go for six. Having reset your elbow and put your leg in a splint, you find a queue of sixteen hot persons awaiting a bath. You lie on your bed and reflect on the injustice and wretchedness of life, and after a considerable period you manage to have a bath. By the time you've finished you find he fresh water has been cut off and you have to shave in tooth water. Also the effort of drying yourself has made you far hotter than you were in the first place. Having decided all you want to do is leave this jot life forever and having cut yourself three times with the razor because you're too weak to control it, you shovel yourself into your shirt and shorts, grab your lifebelt and trail into breakfast. You've been told that its bad to eat too much in hot weather so you just have grapefruit, cornflakes, fish, eggs and bacon and toast and marmalade and coffee, cutting out all the fancy dishes in between.

You now feel so ill and heavy you can hardly drag yourself up to the boat deck. To your delight you find all the deck chairs have been taken so you lean over the side and regard the waves, the fling fish and the rest of the convoy. You remark in monosyllables to your neighbor upon the colour of the sea and how ill you feel. It then becomes necessary o go down below and start queuing again....

About ten o'clock hundreds of bells start ringing. Everyone dons lifebelt and goes to emergency stations. This is lovely – you stand silent and still for forty minutes. Eventually a bugler blows a flat G on his bugle. This heralds the arrival of a curious string of people including the captain, the O.C. Troops, the troops officers, the ship's orderly officer, the orderly chaplain, the orderly doctor, the offices of the guard, the sanitary orderly, the baggage officer, the assistant baggage officer, the entertainment officer, the officer 1/c beer, the quartermaster, the adjutant, and one or two other chaps. They only take about half an hour to get by, but fortunately the bugler can't remember how to blow 'dismiss' so you have the privilege of standing there for another half hour while he racks his brains. The next hour or so is spent in a delightful game specially designed for amusing subalterns. You are told the troop commander wants you in the bowels of the ship. You arrive bathed in sweat. He looks blankly at you and says 'oh he didn't mean you, he really wanted Tom, but as you were there perhaps you'd take a message to the sergeant major'. Good. You stagger up and start trying to find the sergt. Major. He of course knows this perfectly well and has taken the precaution to lock himself up in the hold disguised as a sack of potatoes. You return dispirited to the troop Cds who says, well that being the case perhaps you'd better give the Troops some gun drill. This is enormous fun as the gun, the target and everything else is of course imaginary. You are saved from complete extinction by dissolution into a grease spot, by the fact that someone else arrives and claims the 4 square feet of deck allotted to the battery. You dismiss the men who fall gratefully on the deck and assume attitudes of the dead. You make your way by inches to the Bar and drink a pint of iced lemonade which is probably, you reflect, frightfully bad for you. Good, you think, perhaps I'll die and get thrown into the sea. You pick up a novel and sink into an armchair. You are roused by the adjutant who says Didn't you know you weren't allowed to read novels before lunch? You say yes you did but you thought you'd had lunch, how odd. He looks at you strangely and moves off. You pick up your novel, go to your cabin and continue reading. At one o'clock you eat too large a lunch. Once more you stagger on deck and find no chairs so you lie down on the deck and go to sleep till tea when you are told that you've missed a lecture which you were clearly told to attend yesterday and what dis you mean by it. You burst into loud tears and say you are very unhappy and want your mummy. After tea you feel so awful you think it must be lack of exercise so you play medicine ball and strain your heart, your liver and both wrists. With a feeling of virtue, you have a cold bath. The water no sooner comes in contact with your body than it starts boiling. You get out and lie under a fan and once more hope you'll get a chill and die. At 7 o'clock you eat a 6 course dinner. You go into dinner in sunlight. When you come out it's pitch dark. You can't see a thing and fall over the recumbent forms of a lot of soldiers and sailors strewn around the deck uplifting their melancholy voices in what they fondly imagine to be song. While they express an improbable wish to the only boy in the world, you search frantically for the door. You play pontoon from 8.15 – 10.30 drinking iced orangeade. You decide, when you've reckoned your losses that, thank god, you'll be lucky in love, reflect that, yes it's quite possible and go up on deck for a breather. This is hell. Light and the stars and the convoy gliding on in the moon's light and the phosphorescence in the wash of the ships. You can spend an hour just quietly leaning over the edge and thinking. I have often done so; it's one of the most beautiful, disappointing, perverted and agonizing pictures in the world, these beautiful strong, dark silent ships plying remorselessly purposefully into the night bearing so many men away from their homes, possibly to their death. Then your mood (being young) changes and if the fat little padre leaning over the rail a few feet away were to ask you what you thought of, you would say 'I am thinking of the deck all floodlight; I am thinking of dancing on the deck to "Sand in my shoes" with a girl with laughing blue eyes, to a part of the deck where it's not floodlit. I am thinking of asking her whether she doesn't think the moon is a most beautiful, understanding and wicked woman?"

You descend with your romantic soul, tripping over the bodies, not of cool clean lovers but snoring gunners, and get into or onto bed. You fall into a daze which passes for sleep. At 3 o'clock you are woken by someone who looks at you and says oh he's sorry he thought you were a guard officer tonight. Rather funny, what, he's so very sorry. You say politely it doesn't matter a bit, by all means wake you as often as he likes, it only takes 2 hours to get to sleep again. And so the round begins again, only next day, perhaps you are guard officer and have to get up at 3 and stagger through the ship jumping into hammocks, spans, winches, windlasses, cutlasses, compasses, morasses and molasses.

My dearest, have I bored you? I am well and brown. I have never felt seriously like being sick at all, and I am having, in its way, a good time. The heat makes me feel awfully limp, it's true, but I love just lying on the deck and reading and thinking. I don't miss you because I've never had you to miss except for 2 days some centuries ago, but I miss your letters and hope I shall find a goodly number when I arrive. I get desperate when I think of Scotland and of picnics and Piccadilly, of Surrey and Sussex, of cycling and canoeing and bathing and playing tennis, of gardens and of peaches, or corn on the cob and weddings and bridesmaids of beauty and mirth and Mhairi (pronounced for the sake of alliteration, with an M). Looking back, you see, and looking forward, are bound to be the substitutes. We will have a present together sometime, no matter, as you once said, no matter what happens. We will go, somehow, the Ile aux Moines. What a rash statement! Can't you see the gods laughing to themselves over my presumption? Well if two people's wishes can work anything, we will go there, won't we darling? Utimain te vidisse – if only I had seen you before I left – mais c'est la vie! Goodnight sweetheart, goodnight little independent darling.

John

John Butler

(July 1942) 391/98th Field Regt RA
c/o APO 1755

Alors, ma Cherie, here is the final last letter. It is being written in a luxurious cabin. I am sitting on the lower bunk and my head is pressed against the upper. This is not comfortable. Otherwise we are well off – there are 3 others sharing their cabin. Tom being one thereof.

Thank you for your surprise letter. I am most worried about the odd sounding disease. I haven't the vaguest idea what flebitis is but I do hope you will soon be cured of it. It sounds horrid. Your problem darling of how you could best cross my path is now solved, not alas quite according to plan. This is as one might say, the life.

I have read again John Macnab. I wonder if you know it. It's by John Buchan and is a grand tale of poaching in Scotland. It remindeth me, fair one, of thee. How are you going to send me this much promised photograph? And how changed and different will you be and will I be when it's all over? Don't get married in the meantime my old one.

I am still convinced you're the sweetest fille du monde. Write often et parlez moi d'amour.

Je t'embrasse

John

391/98th 7dRegt R.A.
c/o Army Post Office 1755
August 1942

Dearest,

I am writing largely out of a sense of duty. I have just been censoring some of the men's letters. I do feel sorry for them having to have officers censor their letters, but it is not the most thrilling of occupations for us. The sea, my sweet, is as blue as your eyes and as deep,. This is said with a slight bias. It may be bad security, but I expect the sea is blue everywhere. Tonight is a grand gusty night. You can stand on the deck with the sea wind screaming in your face, (quite friendly and not at all cold), and watch the waves form up and hurl themselves against the side of the ship. They get pushed back and collide with the waves that are following up. The shock causes them, winded, to send up a fine spray which the wind catches and blows in your face. Sometimes a wave crashes up on to the deck. They sea is the most glorious colour, not just blue, but inky and dark and clear and when the foam rolls back from the ship, turquoise. Some days we have had glorious sunshine and lain basking idly, for all the world like a pleasure cruise. In fact the food is grand, better than you can buy at the De Guise I suspect, and certainly more plentiful, and you can dink Brandy @ 6d a glass. We do. At intervals I raise my glass to Vari and my unworthy companions, and I drink your health. Most think, as I in my ignorance once thought, that I refer to some Australia aborigine.

It seems as though I have spent all my life on this ship. Excuse the somewhat irregular shape of this morceau de papier, but I tore it in endeavouring to detach it from the parent block. I wonder if you will ever get this letter. I must say I hate the thought of my words of comfort and grace going to amuse the mermaids.

My dear, it will be so long before we see each other. I have not, contrary to expectations, any great feelings of homesickness (I haven't been seasick either, yet, come to that) but I do sometimes think of what a day it will be when we sail on the return journey into an English port. Perhaps you'll be there to meet me, because there'll be no secret of our arrival. But I probably shouldn't recognize you (aged 30) and how embarrassing it would be. On Monday I am preparing a motion that it is better to have loved and lost than never to have loved at all. I hold very strong opinions on the matter, believe me. This is really quite irrelevant and I'm sure I haven't lost you yet! Have I? (Pathetic cry from lonely soldier. You immediately burst into floods or irremediable tears.) But at any rate it is better to have loved, isn't it? Darling, I am very much hoping that you will send on the much talked of identity disc. This desire arises partly from the sentimentality, which we have so much deplored, and partly from a Big Chief native wallah liking for handing things round the neck, but chiefly, believe me dear, from sentimentality. Besides which it is far more elegant to be buried with a silver disc around one's neck than a cardboard one (or whatever they make army ones from). I like to think, as I spit rhythmically with the rolling of the ship in to the oh so heavenly sea, that you wear the cumbersome and ill engraved medallion in the rough proximity of your heart (If I'm not careful I shall end this letter like this ~~⊕ ⊘~~ ̶x̶ ̶x̶ ̶x̶ ̶x̶ ̶x̶ ̶x̶)

In a fortnight it will be my birthday. You will, I trust, elevate the usual glass of champagne (or was it ginger ale?) to my memory.

Darling, I'm talking rot. I hope to God I come back all in one piece in the not too distant future, to drive you to the Forth Bridge in Marian,(??) to throw pebbles at you in Society, to chink glasses with you at the aperitif, to tread on your toes in the De Guise and fill you with sunshine and seawater in the Ile aux Moines. These lyric thoughts are being hampered by Tom who repeats in monotonous tones "I want to be sick. I think I'm going to be sick."

I spend all my time writing either a diary or the first chapter of my brilliant memoirs of life in the army, entitled Then the Soldier. It is to follow on my unwritten autobiography called as I think I told you, "Infant to Lover". You must write and tell me much more about your acting, your plebiscite of flebitis or whatever it was, because I hate to think of you as being ill, you who are meant to walk and ride and swim, and you must tell of what you are going to do when your term of penance at Ochertyre is up. I shall, you know this, be waiting for your letters where'er I be. I do hope letters don't take more than two years to arrive. Reading all those letters from the men to their wives and girlfriends, it amazes my how uninspiring they are and how unimaginative. We can write letters, Vari, when we're in the mood. However bad citizens we may be.

There's such a hell of a din going on around me that I can't concentrate any more. I am told the post goes very soon, so I think I'd better finish this off. I'll write again to let you know my existence is uninterrupted, and I will continue to lift my glass to you. I shall continue to compare your eyes to the restless ocean and I shall continue to be quite mad and quite inconsequential. It will be nice to touch land again though this voyage is in so many ways a rest cure. Silly mankind – it's never satisfied. There's also a certain pleasure in not having to put a stamp on this!

Au revoir, braw lassie, dinna gorge yersel wi' over mickele Edinburgh rrock, ye ken, t'will gie ye a horrrrrrrible pain, farbye. (??)

With amour and embracement, fare the well my first and fairest,

John

John Butler
c/o APO 1755
August 22nd 1942

Vari dear, I want to write you a very small note in a great hurry just before the post goes.

We have once more re-embarked and are off we know not where.

Vari, I have some news which will maybe make you a little sad. I have gotten myself engaged. I won't try to explain myself or excuse myself or anything. I only hope I have not been unfair to you. That's for you to judge, but I shall write to you form time to time as opportunity permits, and I do want you to write to me. I believe we will be able to do this.

You now see how horribly susceptible
I am – as I always warned you! But please Vari dear, will you wish me luck just as I wish you all the luck. I am very happy, but life being somewhat uncertain at this time, cannot make plans for the future. Forgive this very short note but there is no time for more, and please write and tell me what you think.

With love John

With John's family

391/98th7d Regt R.A.
C/o APO 1755
August 31st 1942

Well, Vari my dear, I am hotter than I have been for about 6 weeks. The sun is beating down on my unprotected head so don't be surprised if I go potty before I've finished. I don't know how many of my letters you have received, but I wrote a week or so ago from our last port of call what must have been a very brief and unsatisfactory note to tell you I was engaged. I'm afraid I had no time for any more.

Well I'll try to enlarge a little and tell you the story. You would, I venture to predict, like Jean. Because she, like you, likes doing silly things, likes music and the countryside and stars and streams and fish and chips. I did tell you, did I not, how hopelessly susceptible I was to your fair sex, and had I met you and known you before I left by vision as well as epistolary communication I should probably have deserted anyway and become a gillie in Scotland.

But Vari, I am really very much in love with Jean, and I think, in fact I'm sure really, that in as many years as I appear likely to spend out in this fever ridden godforsaken part of the world, you will have met and fallen for some glamorous young man who will hear you say horrrrible and fall in love with you. I hope o with all my heart because you are honest and sincere and like all the right things. It is of course quite valueless and impossible to look into the future but I know we'll meet again.

Well I met Jean at a party arranged by a pal of mine and I disliked her intensely. We then went on to dance at a sort of nightclub called The Blue Moon and I changed my opinion quite a lot. After that we used to go out a lot together, dancing at a little place called The Candlelight, walking through heavenly woods up the mountainside where the view was indescribably beautiful. One day we rode, and on our way back we rode straight into the sunset and the distant hills seemed to be far off fairy mountains separated from us by a sea of green mist in which flowers shone brilliant fold. I have never seen such beauty before. We drove about the countryside quite a lot and saw it from every side – the great bays with silver sand and tall mountains, and the rugged heathlands with ling and wild flowers and shrubs stretching for miles to the hills, and the native villages and the clean streets and cities. You can guess where this was but I don't think we're meant to mention it by name.[8] We stayed there over a month and I think it was the most wonderful holiday that I have ever spent. Because it was a holiday, although we used to do a certain amount of training in the mornings.

Everything there is much cheaper than in England – food and of course their own wine which is surprisingly good on the whole and entertainment generally. I suppose it's about

---

[8]   Durban, South Africa

the same as pre-war England but that's so long ago I can't remember. And everybody is unbelievably hospitable. If you walked around looking lost someone was sure to stop their car and take you home to tea and dinner and issue an open invitation. All our chaps I think without exception were taken out by people and send all their spare time at their homes. And everyone is friendly, there's none of the English suspicion or hostility or reserve. Call it which you like. You sit at a table with people in a restaurant and they treat you as if they've known you all your life. The country too is on a much larger scale – it has not the charm of Scotland though it has a different sort of charm – you feel free out there and you can walk and walk and walk without trespassing!

You can imagine how heart-breaking it was when we had to leave though we knew of course it would come soon. We were awfully lucky to spend so may weeks there when most people spend only a few days.

This ship we are on now is a large one and was once luxurious though now somewhat more crowded than erstwhile. It is rolling about quite a bit, but long steady rolls that don't upset the tummy. Unfortunately we all got ptomaine poisoning from some tongue we had for dinner and the whole regiment was in bed for a day. It's the most unpleasant disease and makes your stomach feel like a cauldron of boiling sizzling lead, and it makes you very sick. We haven't really fully recovered yet.

Alors, mon choux, I must terminate this, and wish you a very very happy birthday whether it's still to come, or over some weeks ago. I've no idea how long this'll take to reach you – we've had no mail yet. I hope you'll wish me well, Vari, as I wish you all the happiness there is to find in life, and that's a lot.

With very much love,

John

AFTER

For some reason, I have no more of his wartime letters although we wrote fairly frequently and I have letters from all the rest of his life.

His engagement ended and when we met again in April 1945, we dined and danced as promised but we knew we weren't for each other. I went to his wedding and he came to mine. He and his family visited us and we called on them at Hexham just before they went to live in New Zealand, where he died.

After his memorial service in London, his friend Tom sent me a tape of the service saying that he was the love of my life. I thanked him saying that though he wasn't that, he was my first love – almost as important.

JOHN BUTLER

John Butler, DSO, died on July 25 in Auckland aged 78. He was born in Thames Ditton, Surrey, on July 9, 1920.

IT WAS in Italy in 1943 that John Butler gained that rare distinction among Second World War subalterns: the immediate award of the DSO. His friends in the Surrey and Sussex Yeomanry, with whom he served throughout the war, always considered the decoration to be a "near-miss VC".

In December 1943 Lieutenant Butler, deputising for his wounded troop commander, was acting as forward observation officer for a squadron of a Canadian armoured regiment, which was supporting an attack on German positions on the high ground above the Arielli river in eastern Italy. As the attackers crested the ridge they came under heavy machine-gun and artillery fire and suffered severe casualties.

Butler, after conferring with the tank and infantry commanders, moved his tank back below the crest, and crawled forward to establish an observation post in a wattle hut under continuing shellfire. He had just engaged and silenced two troublesome machine-gun positions and knocked out an enemy OP when a concentration of shells fell on his position, causing heavy infantry casualties and wounding him in the leg. The shelling also cut his radio remote control cable in four places, and on crawling back to his tank to get a spare, he found that his tank had been hit by several shells and his spare sets smashed. Nothing daunted, he arranged to give fire orders by voice control, crawled back to his OP and continued to shoot.

The shelling continued and towards evening he was wounded for a second time, in the shoulder. By now the infantry were withdrawing, but realising that three of them on the forward slope had not heard the order, he crept forward and directed them to withdraw one by one. His movement had brought down a further burst of shellfire, but he persevered and every man reached safety. As night drew on, because of his wounds he was ordered by his battery commander to withdraw. As

Butler in the turret of his observation post tank in the Apennines in 1944

the citation for his DSO stated: "Throughout the day he had manned his OP under constant shellfire, engaging targets with coolness and accuracy and complete disregard of his own personal safety or the wounds he had received. The support he gave both to tanks and infantry was invaluable, and his courage and resource were of the highest order and an outstanding example to the men under his command."

John Close Butler was the youngest child and only son of Harry and Winifred (Bid) Butler of Thames Ditton. He was educated at Aldenham School, where he demonstrated his a strongly independent spirit. This showed when, to the fury of his Headmaster and the amazement of his friends, he suddenly left at Easter 1939, just before his last term when he was to be captain of cricket, to spend three months cycling in France.

In the autumn of 1939 he went to read English at Christ's College, Cambridge. When his studies were interrupted by the war, he was commissioned into the Royal Artillery and posted to the Surrey and Sussex Yeomanry in 1941. He served with the regiment in the Western Desert, Sicily, Italy and finally in Holland and Germany, where he took over command of his battery with the rank of major.

He returned to Cambridge in 1946 and took his degree in the following year. In 1948 he married Philippa Burn and began what looked like a promising career as personnel director with Charringtons in London.

But neither business, nor the pursuit of money suited his nature, which craved travel, outdoor activities and something of a contemplative life away from cities and the rat race. As a result he never had a career or fixed occupation. He resigned from his job in 1955, bought a Land Rover and set out to drive his family through the Levant to Kenya, to farm, being captured by bandits en route. But the farming was not a success, and a year later he returned home across the Sahara. There the Algerian war of independence was in full swing, and he had to join a French military convoy to reach Algiers.

Back in England, after a short apprenticeship, he bought a small mixed farm on Exmoor, where one of his cows nearly ended his days by running her horn right through his thigh as he slipped in the mud while inspecting her calf. So he quitted farming and turned to teaching, ultimately becoming Tutor Organiser for Adult Education in South Warwickshire. But in 1971 some inner "call of the desert" caused him to resign again and to set off with Philippa to view the Palaeolithic cave drawings in the Tibesti Mountains of northern Chad, which rival those of the better known Lascaux caves of south-west France.

Returning again to England they settled in a lonely hilltop dwelling above Nenthead in Northumberland, where he was to spend the next twenty years.

He tried to write, having a great gift of style and humour in his personal letters, which his friends cherished throughout his life. But which he was unable to reproduce this when trying to compose for publication, so he dabbled in a little postal bookselling.

He also spent time making a careful record of the graves in the local cemeteries, brewing his own version of Northumberland ale, and endlessly walking the fells and Hadrian's Wall with his wife. Their wants were simple, even frugal, and walking through Britain became an important part of their life.

By 1994 they realised that they were no longer able to cope with the fells, and after much thought they decided to emigrate to New Zealand, where their daughter and two teenage grandsons were living, and where they could walk the beaches where his ashes are now scattered.

He is survived by his wife, their son and daughter.

Me, now

Lightning Source UK Ltd.
Milton Keynes UK
UKOW02n0620050317
295838UK00002BA/40/P